Predicting Pretrial Failure

How Prior Criminal Record Outperforms Offense Severity

**Enrique Chavez, Stewart J. D'Alessio,
and Lisa Stolzenberg**

ISBN: 978-1-936651-26-9 (paperback)
ISBN: 978-1-936651-27-6 (e-book)

Printed in the United States of America

Use of AI

ChatGPT and Grammarly were used as part of the manuscript development workflow for organizational and editorial support. The authors revised, reviewed and finalized the manuscript and assume full responsibility for its content.

Abstract

Predicting Pretrial Failure: How Prior Criminal Record Outperforms Offense Severity examines one of the most enduring yet least scrutinized assumptions in American pretrial justice: that the statutory seriousness of the current offense is the most appropriate basis for pretrial release decisions. Drawing on data from the State Court Processing Statistics (SCPS) program and decades of empirical research, this book demonstrates that a defendant's prior criminal record—especially the number of prior convictions—is a substantially stronger and more consistent predictor of pretrial failure, defined as pretrial rearrest and failure to appear, than the severity of the current charge. Across multiple logistic regression analyses of felony defendants processed in large urban counties, each additional prior conviction is associated with approximately 11–12% higher odds of pretrial rearrest and approximately 6% higher odds of failure to appear, net of offense severity and other legal and extralegal controls. These findings call into question the continued reliance on charge-based bail schedules, which dominate contemporary practice despite their weak empirical grounding, limited relationship to actual pretrial risk, and disproportionate impact on economically disadvantaged defendants and communities of color.

Beyond the statistical evidence, the book situates pretrial decision-making within the broader historical, constitutional, and sociopolitical context of bail in the United States. Chapters trace the evolution of bail from its Anglo-Saxon origins to modern preventive detention, analyze Supreme Court jurisprudence that has shaped the Eighth Amendment's prohibition on excessive bail, and examine in detail how cash bail produces wealth-based detention, coerced guilty pleas, racial inequality, and long-term socioeconomic harms. The book integrates research on jail conditions, mental health consequences, employment disruption, stigma, case outcomes, and the collateral effects of pretrial detention—demonstrating that even short periods of pretrial confinement can generate profound and lasting consequences for defendants, their families, and their communities.

This work also reviews constitutional challenges to fixed bail schedules, the Department of Justice's growing concern with wealth-based detention, and the emergence—and limitations—of contemporary algorithmic risk-assessment tools. By synthesizing legal analysis, quantitative evidence, and policy scholarship, the book argues for a pretrial system grounded in empirically validated risk indicators rather than tradition, intuition, or economic capacity. It concludes by outlining concrete policy reforms, including constraining the routine use of monetary bail, integrating criminal history more centrally into pretrial decision-making frameworks, enhancing access to counsel at bail hearings, and expanding non-monetary release options that promote public safety while honoring constitutional principles.

Ultimately, *Predicting Pretrial Failure* demonstrates that meaningful pretrial reform cannot occur without recognizing the central—and empirically supported—role of prior criminal records in predicting pretrial behavior. In doing so, the book offers a scientifically rigorous, constitutionally grounded, and policy-relevant blueprint for reshaping one of the most consequential stages of the American criminal justice process.

Table of Contents

Chapter 1:

Pretrial Justice in America

In 2020, the United States' carceral system experienced one of the most consequential shocks in its modern history. Bail reform—long a subject of scholarly and policy debate but unevenly implemented—moved to the forefront of national attention following the arrest and death of George Floyd. Millions of people took to the streets in all fifty states, giving unprecedented visibility to longstanding criticisms of the American criminal justice system (Ansel, 2021). Although the Floyd case most directly exposed systemic racism (Moody-Ramirez et al., 2021) and patterns of excessive force in policing (Pryce & Gainey, 2022), it also intensified scrutiny of pretrial justice, particularly the role of cash bail in producing mass pretrial detention and its disproportionate impact on Black and Brown communities.

Contemporary debates about pretrial detention unfold within what Campbell and Vogel (2019) describe as a broader "demographic divide," in which generational differences in ideology and perceptions of public safety produce competing understandings of risk following arrest. In such a politically charged environment, decisions about who should be confined and who should be released before trial cannot sensibly be guided by shifting public sentiment, media-driven moral panics, or reflexively punitive responses to crime waves. Instead, they require a principled decision-making framework grounded in equity and predictive accuracy: similarly situated defendants should be treated alike, and assessments of pretrial risk should rest on empirically validated indicators rather than intuition, stereotypes, or financial resources.

The scale of pretrial detention underscores the urgency of this task. On any given day, local jails in the United States hold nearly half a million individuals, more than half of whom have not been convicted and are legally presumed innocent (Yang, 2017). A substantial body of research documents the wide-ranging consequences of bail and pretrial detention, including effects on crime rates (Rose & Shem-Tov, 2021), rehabilitation and desistance (Dabney et al., 2017), jail overcrowding and mass incarceration (Wilson, 2022), and racial inequality in pretrial outcomes (Bearfield et al., 2023). Yet the central problem confronting contemporary bail systems is not only the downstream harms of detention, but the criteria by which pretrial release decisions are made in the first place. Pretrial detention based on poorly calibrated or incomplete risk indicators conflicts with both the presumption of innocence and democratic ideals of personal liberty. As Aristotle observed, a core promise of democracy is the opportunity "to be ruled and to rule in turn, and to live as one chooses"—a condition that is denied to those confined without adequate justification (Hansen, 2010, p. 11).

This book contributes to ongoing reform efforts by examining the role of a defendant's prior criminal record in predicting pretrial failure, defined as pretrial rearrest and failure to appear. An extensive body of research has established the enduring consequences of criminal records, demonstrating that prior convictions generate employer stigma during hiring (Lageson et al., 2015), restrict employment opportunities (Denver et al., 2018), limit access to housing and public benefits (Gustafson, 2011), and reduce civic participation, including voting and community engagement (McEachin et al., 2020). If prior criminal history proves to be a stronger and more consistent predictor of pretrial failure than the statutory severity of the current charge—even after accounting for legally relevant controls—important policy implications follow. Community safety may be better served by constraining the routine use of monetary bail, which frequently functions as a wealth-based screening mechanism, and by placing greater weight on empirically grounded risk indicators, particularly criminal history.

Legally, the state is permitted to consider a defendant's criminal record in assessing both danger to the community and likelihood of flight. Practically, a pretrial system that emphasizes prior record offers advantages over more complex actuarial instruments: criminal history is routinely collected, standardized across jurisdictions, and readily interpretable by justice officials. This raises a central policy question: who truly requires pretrial incapacitation? When pretrial decisions are anchored in empirically validated indicators of risk rather than the seriousness of the presenting charge or the defendant's ability to pay, fewer individuals will be detained for reasons unrelated to public safety, and the administration of justice will move closer to the constitutional ideals of fairness, proportionality, and equal treatment under law.

Jail Incarceration in the United States

The United States maintains three primary correctional systems— local jails and state and federal prisons—which together confine roughly 2.2 million individuals on an average day (Kaeble & Cowhig, 2018). Local jails, which account for about 30% of the incarcerated population, typically house individuals serving short sentences for misdemeanors or low-level felonies, as well as those held pretrial. State prisons hold approximately 61% of incarcerated people, and federal institutions hold the remaining 9% (Kaeble & Cowhig, 2018). Despite comprising only about 5% of the world's population, the United States incarcerates nearly a quarter of the world's prisoners, making it a global outlier in the use of confinement (Davis, 2022).

Recent data highlight both the scale and volatility of jail incarceration. In 2020, state and federal prisons held 1,215,800 individuals, while local jails confined approximately 549,100 people at midyear (Zeng, 2022). The jail count represents a substantial decline from the previous year, mainly attributable to pandemic-era decarceration initiatives, temporary court closures, and reductions in new admissions. Yet, even during periods of decline, the basic composition of jail populations has remained remarkably stable: roughly two-thirds of individuals held in jails have not been convicted of a crime and are detained solely because their cases are pending (Davis, 2022). The United States thus stands alone in its reliance on pretrial detention, confining nearly half a million people daily—almost twice as many as any other country (Fair & Walmsley, 2016). Chronic overcrowding further strains local jail systems: the average nationwide jail capacity is approximately 84%, and some jurisdictions, including portions of California, operate at more than 100% of rated capacity (Coggins, 2020).

A key institutional driver of jail growth has been the expanded use of cash bail and the concurrent decline in release on recognizance (Bechtel et al., 2012). Between 1970 and 2015, the number of individuals held pretrial increased more than fivefold, from 82,922 to 441,790 (Digard & Swavola, 2019). This growth has occurred despite the fact that most defendants lack the financial resources to satisfy even relatively modest bail amounts. Reaves (2013) reports that nearly 90% of defendants are unable to pay the bond premiums required for release. Judges frequently set bail near $10,000, yet 40% of Americans cannot cover an unexpected $400 expense (Dobbie & Yang, 2021). Consistent with these constraints, many pretrial detainees have weak attachment to the formal labor market. Dobbie et al. (2018) found that only 32% of defendants jailed in Miami and Philadelphia were employed in the year preceding arrest, with average annual earnings of $4,524.

The reach of incarceration has become so extensive that it reshapes national demographic trajectories. Nearly as many men are released from prison each year as graduate from college (Massoglia & Pridemore, 2015). For African American men born since the late 1960s, serving time in prison is now more common than completing a four-year college degree (Travis et al., 2014). A substantial body of research further demonstrates that race—closely intertwined with socioeconomic status—profoundly shapes both the likelihood of being granted bail and the capacity to afford it (Monaghan et al., 2022).

The burdens of the cash bail system fall most heavily on economically disadvantaged defendants, particularly Black men. Persistent income disparities magnify these effects. Using nationally representative labor-market data, Wilson and Darity Jr. (2022) show that in 2019 Black male wage earners earned 24.4% less per hour than White male wage earners; even after accounting for education, state of residence, and work experience, a 14.9% wage gap remained, reflecting structural labor-market inequality rather than job mismatch. In addition, Black unemployment rates have historically been approximately twice those of Whites. These economic disadvantages substantially increase the difficulty of posting bail (Wooldredge et al., 2015) or retaining private counsel. As a result, Black defendants are less likely to engage in early plea bargaining and more likely to proceed to trial, a pattern associated with harsher sentencing outcomes following conviction (Donnelly & MacDonald, 2018).

Policymakers recognized the inequities of bail long before the latest wave of reform. At the signing of the Bail Reform Act of 1966, President Lyndon B. Johnson captured the enduring moral tension at the heart of the system:

The defendant with means can afford to pay bail. He can afford to buy his freedom. But the poorer defendant cannot pay the price. He languishes in jail for weeks, months, and perhaps even years before trial. He does not stay in jail because he is guilty. He does not stay in jail because any sentence has been passed. He does not stay in jail because he is any more likely to flee before trial. He stays in jail for one reason only: he stays in jail because he is poor.

(Dobbie et al., 2018, p. 201)

More than half a century later, Johnson's critique remains disturbingly accurate. The contemporary structure of cash bail continues to produce a two-tiered system of justice in which pretrial liberty depends more heavily on financial capacity than on legally relevant assessments of risk or fairness.

Changes in the U.S. Jail Population

U.S. Jail Population and Incarceration Rate

Over the past 150 years, the U.S. jail population has increased dramatically, with the most rapid growth occurring in the late twentieth century. During the late nineteenth and early twentieth centuries, incarceration rates were relatively low, reflecting a less centralized and less punitive approach to crime control (Cahalan, 1986). For much of the early and mid-twentieth century, jail populations remained relatively stable, in part because crime rates were lower and pretrial practices were more discretionary and less formally structured (Clear, 2007).

A profound shift began in the early 1970s, marking the onset of what scholars often describe as the era of mass incarceration. Jail and prison populations expanded sharply in response to a combination of policy developments, including mandatory sentencing statutes, habitual offender laws, intensified drug enforcement, and the political embrace of "tough on crime" rhetoric (Clear, 2007). Local jails, once primarily short-term holding facilities, increasingly became central components of a broader punitive system. By the end of the twentieth century, the United States had emerged as the world's leading incarcerator, prompting sustained concern about proportionality, racial disparities, and the long-term social and economic consequences of widespread confinement (Western, 2006).

Historical estimates illustrate the magnitude of this transformation. In 1880, roughly 18,686 individuals were held in local jails, producing an incarceration rate of 37 per 100,000 residents (Cahalan, 1986). By 1970, the jail population had risen to more than 160,000, and by the early 1980s it exceeded 220,000. This upward trajectory continued throughout the late twentieth century, with the jail population surpassing 250,000 in the mid-1980s, 400,000 by 1990, 500,000 by the mid-1990s, and more than 620,000 by 2000 (Minton, 2011). The growth was not merely numerical. Incarceration rates more than doubled between the early 1980s and mid-2000s, increasing from fewer than 100 jail inmates per 100,000 residents to more than 250 per 100,000 (Minton & Zeng, 2021).

The jail population peaked around 2010 at nearly 750,000 individuals, with an incarceration rate of approximately 242 per 100,000 residents. This peak reflected a long-term shift from relatively limited jail use to the institutional centrality of jails within the broader system of mass incarceration. Much of this growth coincided with aggressive drug enforcement, routine reliance on pretrial detention following arrest, and the expanding use of cash bail (Subramanian et al., 2015).

After 2010, the jail population declined modestly, falling to approximately 721,000 by 2015, with a corresponding reduction in the incarceration rate to about 230 per 100,000 (Minton & Zeng, 2016). A more dramatic contraction occurred in 2020, when the jail population dropped to roughly 549,000 and the rate to about 167 per 100,000—a decrease of nearly 38% relative to the mid-2000s peak (Minton & Zeng, 2021). This abrupt decline was driven primarily by the COVID-19 pandemic, which produced emergency decarceration measures, curtailed court operations, and temporarily reduced new admissions.

These declines, however, did not represent a fundamental reversal of long-term trends. By 2021, jail counts had already begun to rebound, increasing by more than 87,000 to approximately 636,300, with the incarceration rate rising to nearly 192 per 100,000 (Zeng, 2022). The speed of this rebound illustrates the structural resilience of contemporary incarceration practices once external pressures subside.

Taken together, these trends document a profound transformation in the function of local jails—from relatively modest, community-based holding facilities into central institutions within a national system of mass incarceration and pretrial detention. Whether the public safety benefits of this expansion justify its economic, social, and constitutional costs remains a central question in contemporary criminal justice policy (Clear, 2007).

Convicted versus Unconvicted

Understanding the evolving composition of jail populations is essential for interpreting long-term incarceration trends and for evaluating the role of pretrial decision-making in contemporary criminal justice. Local jails house both convicted individuals—those serving short sentences, awaiting sentencing, or detained for violations of probation or parole—and unconvicted individuals, who are detained while awaiting arraignment, trial, or other court proceedings and who are legally presumed innocent (Gilliard & Beck, 1996). This dual function places jails at the intersection of sentencing policy and pretrial release practices.

In the mid-1980s, roughly half of all jail inmates were convicted, and half were unconvicted. Baunach and Kline (1987) reported that, in 1984, approximately 48% of jail inmates were serving sentences or otherwise convicted, while 52% were awaiting case disposition. Although both groups expanded over the next decade, the unconvicted population grew more rapidly. By 1990, Stephan and Jankowski (1991) found that unconvicted individuals constituted a slight majority of the jail population, underscoring the growing centrality of pretrial detention in local correctional practice.

The expansion of pretrial detention continued through the mid-1990s. Gilliard and Beck (1996) reported that by 1995 the number of convicted inmates had risen by nearly 100,000 relative to 1985 levels, while the unconvicted population had approximately doubled, reaching more than 280,000 individuals. These increases reflected expanded felony caseloads, intensified drug enforcement, longer case-processing times, and the growing reliance on financial bail schedules that restricted release options for economically disadvantaged defendants.

Between the mid-1980s and 2005, the unconvicted population increased steadily, while the number of convicted inmates changed more modestly. Harrison and Beck (2006) documented a 6% decline in the convicted jail population between 1995 and 2005, indicating that much of the overall expansion in jail use during this period was driven by growth in pretrial detention rather than by short-term sentenced confinement. By 2010, Minton (2011) reported that approximately six of ten jail inmates were convicted and four of ten were unconvicted, proportions that had remained relatively stable since 2005, yet continued to reflect substantial reliance on pretrial detention.

The arrival of the COVID-19 pandemic produced significant, though temporary, shifts in jail populations. Minton and Zeng (2021) found that from mid-2019 to mid-2020, the number of inmates in custody who were convicted declined by approximately 34%, while the unconvicted population fell by roughly 21%. These changes resulted from decarceration efforts, court shutdowns, altered arrest practices, and reduced new admissions. As courts reopened and enforcement patterns returned to normal in 2021, both the convicted and unconvicted segments of the jail population increased once again (Zeng, 2022).

Taken together, these historical patterns demonstrate that unconvicted individuals have consistently constituted a substantial—and often dominant—share of the jail population. This persistent reliance on pretrial detention underscores the importance of scrutinizing bail practices, financial conditions of release, and the structural inequalities that shape who remains confined prior to adjudication.

Sex and the U.S. Jail Population

The U.S. jail population has long exhibited a pronounced gender imbalance. Western and Pettit (2010) observe that jails are overwhelmingly male institutions, with men consistently comprising close to 90% of those incarcerated. Yet despite this persistent dominance, women's incarceration in jails has increased markedly over the past several decades, reflecting shifts in enforcement priorities, drug policy, and the social conditions of women situated at the margins of the criminal legal system.

Early national assessments indicated that female incarceration was increasing at a faster rate than male incarceration. Stephan (1984) reported that the number of women in jails increased by 65% during a single survey period, compared with a 40% increase for men. Although women still constituted a small minority of jail inmates, their more rapid growth signaled an important transformation in the gender composition of local jail populations.

In absolute terms, the male jail population expanded from fewer than 250,000 in the mid-1980s to more than 650,000 by 2010—an increase of approximately 178%. After 2010, male jail counts declined modestly, falling to about 624,000 by 2015 and to just under 480,000 in 2020. These reductions reflected a combination of policy reforms, shifts in policing strategies, and the extraordinary disruptions produced by the COVID-19 pandemic (Minton & Zeng, 2021).

Female incarceration followed a distinct yet parallel trajectory. The number of women in jails increased from approximately 19,000 in 1985 to more than 94,000 by 2005—an increase of roughly 396%. The female jail population declined slightly in 2010, rose again by 2015 to more than 100,000, and then fell sharply to around 70,000 in 2020 (Minton & Zeng, 2021). The long-term growth in women's incarceration has been linked to intensified drug law enforcement, heightened surveillance of low-income women, and stricter enforcement of community supervision conditions. The more recent decline is attributable primarily to pandemic-related reductions in admissions and emergency decarceration efforts.

Across the past four decades, men have consistently constituted the overwhelming majority of the jail population in the United States. Throughout this period, men have typically accounted for roughly 85-93% of jail inmates, while women have comprised a much smaller but gradually increasing share. In the mid-1980s, women accounted for approximately 7% of the jail population. By the 1990s and early 2000s, that share had risen into the low double digits, generally ranging between 10 and 12%, reflecting broader changes in policing, prosecution, and sentencing practices affecting women. More recently, the gender composition of jails has remained relatively stable, with women comprising approximately 12-14% of inmates in most years. Notably, however, the COVID-19 pandemic produced an unprecedented contraction in jail populations, including a 37% decline in the number of incarcerated women between 2019 and 2020 (Minton & Zeng, 2021).

Taken together, these trends demonstrate that although jails remain predominantly male institutions, the long-term increase and recent volatility in women's incarceration represent one of the most significant demographic shifts in the contemporary jail population. These patterns underscore the importance of examining gender-specific pathways into the criminal justice system and developing policies, health services, and reentry supports that respond to the distinct experiences and needs of both men and women.

Race and the U.S. Jail Population

Racial disparities have been a defining feature of incarceration in the United States. Beyond the sheer scale of confinement, the disproportionate representation of Black Americans in jails constitutes one of the most pressing criminal justice issues of the modern era (Tonry, 1994). Historical and contemporary data demonstrate the persistence of these disparities and reveal how the demographic composition of jail populations reflects broader inequalities in policing, prosecution, and socioeconomic conditions.

In the mid-1980s, Baunach and Kline (1987) reported that White individuals accounted for 59% of the jail population, Black individuals for 40%, and all other racial groups for approximately 1%. Hispanic inmates comprised about 14% of the total, although they were often treated as a racial rather than an ethnic category in official statistics.

By 1990, Stephan and Jankowski (1991) found that White inmates represented 51% of the jail population, Black inmates 47%, and other inmates 2%, with Hispanic inmates again constituting roughly 14%. These early estimates highlight both the substantial representation of Black Americans in jails and the limitations of historical data, which frequently conflated race and ethnicity.

More recent surveys from the Bureau of Justice Statistics reveal both continuity and change. In 1995, Black Americans constituted approximately 43 to 44% of the jail population—the largest share of any racial group. Over the next two decades, their representation gradually declined, reaching about 35% by 2015 and remaining at a similar level in 2020 (Minton & Zeng, 2021). Although this decline reflects some shift in proportional representation, Black Americans remain dramatically overrepresented relative to their share of the general population.

White incarceration followed a different pattern. White inmates made up about 40% of the jail population in 1995, a smaller share than Black inmates at that time. Beginning in the mid-2000s, however, the proportion of White inmates in jails increased, reaching approximately 44% in 2005 and 2010 and nearly 48% by 2015, before stabilizing at roughly 48% in 2020. These changes indicate a gradual narrowing of the proportional gap between White and Black jail populations, even as both groups continue to be heavily affected by local incarceration (Minton & Zeng, 2021).

Hispanic representation in jails has remained relatively stable across survey years, fluctuating between approximately 14 and 16%. Although Hispanics constitute an ethnic rather than a racial category, BJS surveys between 1995 and 2020 often reported them alongside racial classifications. Their persistent overrepresentation reflects the intersecting effects of socioeconomic disadvantage, differential enforcement practices, and immigration-related criminalization (Harrison & Beck, 2006).

Individuals classified as "other races"—including American Indian or Alaska Native, Asian, Native Hawaiian, and Pacific Islander—have comprised a small but enduring share of the jail population, typically between 1 and 2%. Those categorized as "two or more races" account for an even smaller proportion, rarely exceeding 1%. Although small, these groups may exhibit distinct patterns of surveillance and criminalization that are not readily captured in aggregate statistics.

It is essential to distinguish between representation within the jail population and incarceration rates. The proportions reported above indicate each group's share of those confined but do not reflect the incarceration rate of group members relative to their population size. Contemporary analyses demonstrate that White incarceration is underrepresented relative to population share, whereas Black, Hispanic, and Native American incarceration is substantially overrepresented, reflecting persistent racial inequities at every stage of the criminal process—from policing and charging through sentencing and reentry (Sawyer & Wagner, 2023).

Taken together, these patterns indicate that despite some proportional shifts over time, the overrepresentation of Black and Hispanic individuals remains a defining feature of local jail incarceration. Any meaningful effort to reform pretrial justice must confront these racialized patterns and the structural inequalities that generate and sustain them.

Bail in the United States

Bail is the conditional release of an accused person prior to trial, typically secured by a financial bond that guarantees appearance in court. In common-law systems, including the United States, the historical purpose of bail has been to avoid unnecessary pretrial detention by using money, property, or human sureties as guarantees of future compliance. The modern bail system is generally understood to serve two primary objectives: ensuring that defendants return for scheduled court appearances and reducing the likelihood of new criminal activity during the pretrial period (Zottola et al., 2021). These objectives must be balanced against constitutional and moral constraints, including prohibitions on excessive bail and the principle that liberty should not be restricted more than necessary to protect public interests. In practice, however, contemporary bail practices have been profoundly shaped by social and economic inequalities, producing a system in which defendants from marginalized communities are more likely to be detained and to experience the pretrial process as a form of financial extraction rather than adjudicative fairness.

The practical administration of bail creates substantial opportunities for delay and disparity. Allen (2016) reports that thousands of individuals wait more than 48 hours before appearing before a judicial officer who determines their conditions of release. In many jurisdictions, bail schedules—standardized monetary amounts assigned to specific charges—are employed to streamline decisions and promote administrative uniformity. Although intended to enhance efficiency, these schedules frequently operate as an arrest tax that disproportionately burdens economically disadvantaged and minority defendants, while doing little to improve the accuracy of pretrial risk assessment.

Florida illustrates many of these patterns. All but one of its judicial circuits rely on bail schedules to establish monetary conditions of release (Mitchell et al., 2022). When schedules are not applied, judges conduct individualized assessments that weigh risks of flight and threats to public safety. Defendants deemed low risk may be released on their own recognizance, meaning they are released based solely on their promise to appear for scheduled court proceedings. Others may be subject to non-monetary conditions, including restrictions on new law violations, electronic monitoring, drug or alcohol testing, employment or schooling requirements, or participation in substance use or mental health treatment (Carroll, 2021). Individuals assessed as higher risk may be required to post monetary bail or may be denied bail altogether. Research further indicates that judicial discretion in bail determinations is not immune from disparity: judges' race and sex have been linked to differences in punishment severity, decision speed, and legal outcomes (Boyd, 2016).

When monetary bail is imposed, defendants who can afford to pay the full amount directly to the court are released and receive a refund at the conclusion of the case, provided they comply with court obligations. Those unable to pay typically turn to commercial bail bond agents, who charge nonrefundable premiums—commonly around 10% of the total bail amount—and may require collateral such as property or valuables (Liu et al., 2018). Both the defendant and a cosigner may be subject to background and credit checks. If the defendant fails to appear, the bond company becomes financially liable for the full bail amount and may seize any posted collateral. For certain serious offenses, such as first- or second-degree homicide, bail may be categorically denied. In other cases, judges may deny bail if they determine that no set of conditions would reasonably ensure appearance or protect public safety (Dobbie et al., 2018).

Despite bail's central role in the criminal process, scholars observe that its modern purpose remains contested. On one hand, bail is intended to safeguard the right to due process by preventing punishment prior to conviction and enabling defendants to participate meaningfully in their defense while remaining in the community (Carroll, 2020). On the other hand, bail is frequently used to manage perceived public-safety risks, even when those risks are only loosely related to the financial conditions imposed. The result is a system that formally honors the presumption of innocence while often penalizing those who lack the financial means to secure release. A growing body of research demonstrates that pretrial detention is strongly associated with adverse case outcomes: defendants who remain in jail are more likely to be convicted, to receive custodial sentences, and to receive longer imprisonment terms (Louis, 2022). These findings underscore the significant influence of bail decisions on individual life trajectories and community well-being.

Origins of Bail

Understanding the historical development of bail is essential for evaluating contemporary reform efforts. While practices resembling surety arrangements can be traced to ancient Rome and even to Old Testament references (Wilson, 1925), the foundational principles of American bail are rooted primarily in English common law (Schnacke, 2014). Following the collapse of the Roman Empire in the fifth century, Germanic tribes such as the Angles, Saxons, and Jutes settled in Britain, and their customary practices exerted a lasting influence on early Anglo-Saxon legal institutions.

In these early societies, blood feuds served as the principal mechanism for resolving wrongdoing. Conflicts between families were addressed through retaliatory violence that could extend across generations (Scott-Hayward & Fradella, 2019). Over time, these practices evolved into a compensation-based system known as wergeld. Under this framework, offenders or their families paid monetary compensation: a "wergeld" for homicide, a "bot" for property or personal injury, or a "wile" for fines owed to the monarch. Compensation levels varied according to the social rank of both victim and offender (Scott-Hayward & Fradella, 2019). Unlike modern criminal justice systems, which treat offenses as wrongs against the state, the wergeld system conceptualized wrongdoing as a private matter to be resolved between families.

To ensure that accused individuals appeared for adjudication and satisfied the required compensation, Anglo-Saxon law developed the institution of suretyship. A family member or community representative pledged to guarantee the accused's appearance, initially risking physical punishment and later financial liability if the accused failed to appear (Gross, 2018). This system closely resembles modern unsecured bonds, in which cosigners assume financial responsibility if defendants abscond. Under the Anglo-Saxon model, the bail amount typically corresponded to the expected fine, thereby aligning the security with the anticipated penalty (Schnacke, 2014).

The Norman Conquest of 1066 introduced substantial transformations to English criminal law. Three developments were particularly consequential. First, certain offenses were reclassified as "crimes of royal concern," placing them under direct authority of the Crown. Second, the presentment jury emerged, empowering community members to initiate accusations based on suspicion. Third, royal justices began traveling across the kingdom, promoting centralization and legal uniformity (Schnacke, 2014). These changes contributed to the expansion of jails, which housed individuals accused of violating royal law while awaiting judgment. As punishments became more severe and trial delays lengthened, sheriffs increasingly relied on sureties to secure release and guarantee payment if defendants failed to appear (Seibler & Snead, 2017). Although initially all offenses were bailable, the Assize of Clarendon in 1166 designated certain serious crimes, including murder and forest violations, as nonbailable and formalized the role of presentment juries (Scott-Hayward & Fradella, 2019).

As sheriffs acquired broad discretion to set bail and choose between detention and release, opportunities for corruption multiplied, prompting successive legal reforms. A pivotal development occurred with the Statute of Westminster of 1275, which codified existing law and established a more regulated bail system. The statute required bail decisions to consider the nature of the offense, the strength of evidence and likelihood of conviction, and the accused's prior criminal record (Schnacke et al., 2010). These provisions constrained sheriffs' authority and created a structured bail framework that remained influential for nearly five centuries.

Subsequent legal reforms further limited abuses in pretrial detention. The Petition of Right of 1628 prohibited imprisonment without a stated charge; the Habeas Corpus Act of 1679 mandated prompt judicial review and established procedures to prevent unlawful detention; and the English Bill of Rights of 1689 explicitly prohibited the imposition of excessive bail (Seibler & Snead, 2017). Although these reforms strengthened protections for accused individuals, they did not establish an absolute right to bail in all cases (Seibler & Snead, 2017).

English bail principles were later transplanted into American colonial law. Many colonies modeled their legal codes on British statutes, while others incorporated English legal philosophy into colonial charters (Schnacke et al., 2010). Even before the Habeas Corpus Act and the English Bill of Rights, Massachusetts adopted the 1641 Body of Liberties, guaranteeing bail in noncapital cases (Schnacke et al., 2010). In 1645, the Virginia Colony enacted legislation holding sheriffs civilly liable for failing to take sufficient bail (Seibler & Snead, 2017). These provisions effectively established a presumption of bail for all noncapital offenses.

Pennsylvania's 1682 statute further expanded bail protections by guaranteeing release in all cases except for capital offenses where evidence strongly indicated guilt (Schnacke et al., 2010). This framework influenced many state constitutions drafted after 1776, which incorporated explicit bail provisions in their declarations of rights. For example, the 1776 Virginia Declaration of Rights stated that "excessive bail ought not to be required," echoing the English Bill of Rights. Nevertheless, even after independence, a uniform right to bail in all cases did not exist; legislatures retained authority to designate which offenses were bailable, and courts continued to exercise substantial discretion.

Bail and the U.S. Constitution

The development of bail law in the United States reflects both its English origins and distinct American concerns about liberty, equality, and governmental power. Drawing on the language of the Virginia Declaration of Rights, the First Congress adopted the Eighth Amendment in 1789, declaring that "excessive bail shall not be required, nor excessive fines imposed, nor cruel and unusual punishments inflicted." This clause established an enduring constitutional constraint on state authority and expressed a foundational commitment to protecting individuals from arbitrary pretrial detention.

Soon thereafter, Congress enacted the Judiciary Act of 1789, formally establishing the federal right to bail:

Upon all arrests in criminal cases, bail shall be admitted, except where the punishment may be death, in which cases, it shall not be admitted but by the Supreme Court or a Circuit Court, or by a Justice of the Supreme Court or a Judge of a District Court, who shall exercise their discretion regarding the nature and circumstances of the offense, the evidence, and the usages of law.

(Hegreness, 2013, p. 949)

This statutory framework aligned with the framers' intent by limiting excessive bail and creating a default presumption of release in noncapital cases. As Seibler and Snead (2017) observe, federal law has historically reinforced state constitutional protections by recognizing the right to bail, preserving legislative authority over bail eligibility, and restricting the imposition of unreasonable monetary conditions.

The American context, however, introduced practical challenges. Vast territories and sparse populations increased the risk of flight and reduced the availability of personal sureties. Over time, the function of sureties shifted from physically ensuring a defendant's appearance to guaranteeing payment in the event of nonappearance. This transformation enabled commercial bail, as private actors began underwriting it for profit. Courts facilitated this development by refunding forfeitures when bondsmen demonstrated good-faith efforts to locate absconding defendants.

The modern commercial bail bond industry emerged in the late nineteenth century. In 1896, the McDonough brothers began underwriting bail bonds in San Francisco, establishing the first major commercial bail enterprise in the United States (Dabney et al., 2017). Although their firm dominated the industry for decades, it became synonymous with corruption and exploitation, prompting increased regulatory oversight (Feeley, 1983). Despite these concerns, commercial bail remains central to pretrial release in most jurisdictions today.

By the mid-twentieth century, empirical research had documented the persistent disadvantage experienced by individuals living in poverty who were unable to purchase their freedom (Schnacke et al., 2010). These findings catalyzed what scholars describe as three generations of modern bail reform (Garrett, 2022).

The first generation, beginning in the 1950s, sought to replace rigid bail schedules with individualized hearings focused on flight risk. A landmark decision in this era was Stack v. Boyle (1951), in which the Supreme Court held that bail must be tailored to individual circumstances and that bail set higher than necessary to ensure appearance violates the Eighth Amendment. This period also witnessed experimentation with nonfinancial release alternatives. The Manhattan Bail Project, launched in 1961 by the Vera Institute of Justice and the New York University School of Law, assessed defendants' community ties—such as employment, residence, and family relationships—to estimate the likelihood of court appearance and recommended release on recognizance when appropriate. Fewer than 1% of participants failed to appear, demonstrating that financial conditions were not necessary to ensure compliance (Stemen & Olson, 2023).

These results informed the enactment of the Bail Reform Act of 1966, which codified the principle that individuals should not be detained solely because they are unable to pay. The Act required release on personal recognizance or unsecured bond in noncapital cases unless a judge determined that such release would not reasonably assure appearance (Gross, 2018). Judges were instructed to consider factors such as the nature of the offense, the strength of the evidence, family and community ties, employment, financial resources, mental condition, and prior appearance history (Henning, 2022). President Lyndon B. Johnson summarized the statute's animating concern when he observed that for too long "the scales of justice have been weighted...with money" (Garrett, 2022, p. 888).

The 1966 framework, however, focused primarily on flight risk and did not explicitly authorize detention on public-safety grounds. Rising concerns about violent crime in the 1970s produced a second generation of bail reform emphasizing dangerousness. The District of Columbia Court Reform and Criminal Procedure Act of 1970 authorized pretrial detention in noncapital cases on public-safety grounds (Dabney et al., 2017), and many states soon adopted similar provisions (Koepke & Robinson, 2018).

Federal bail law was again substantially revised with the Bail Reform Act of 1984, which formally authorized preventive detention. Judges could deny bail upon clear and convincing evidence that a defendant posed a danger to the community or a serious risk of flight (Zottola et al., 2021). The statute also established rebuttable presumptions of detention for specified serious offenses (18 U.S.C. § 3142(e)). In United States v. Salerno (1987), the Supreme Court upheld the constitutionality of preventive detention, concluding that when Congress mandates detention based on a compelling governmental interest other than flight prevention, the Eighth Amendment does not require release on bail (pp. 754–755). After Salerno, most states codified public safety and flight risk as central considerations in bail decisions (Schnacke et al., 2010). Yet, as Henning (2022) observes, the Court left unresolved the meaning of "excessive" bail, thereby preserving broad discretion to impose monetary conditions that effectively detain defendants without formally denying bail.

A third generation of reform, emerging in the early twenty-first century, introduced actuarial pretrial risk assessment instruments. Approximately fourteen states and numerous local jurisdictions now employ such tools, which use variables such as prior convictions, pending charges, failure-to-appear history, and indicators of instability to estimate the likelihood of missed court appearances or new criminal activity (Jannetta & Duane, 2022). One prominent example is the Virginia Pretrial Risk Assessment Instrument (VPRAI), which assigns defendants a score from 1 to 9, with lower scores indicating suitability for recognizance release and higher scores suggesting the need for supervision or restrictive conditions (Barno et al., 2020).

Although risk assessment tools aim to reduce reliance on monetary bail and promote consistency, they have generated substantial debate. Critics contend that these instruments reproduce racial disparities because they rely on criminal justice data shaped by historically biased policing and prosecution practices, and that they may overestimate the risk of pretrial failure (Moore, 2022). Supporters argue that when carefully designed, transparently implemented, and regularly audited, such tools can reduce unnecessary detention and diminish the influence of wealth on pretrial liberty (Lowder et al., 2021). Nonetheless, even proponents acknowledge that all risk assessment remains probabilistic and subject to prediction error.

Against this historical and institutional backdrop, the present study addresses a central empirical question: whether and to what extent a defendant's prior criminal record predicts pretrial failure, and how its predictive power compares with the statutory severity of the charged offense. By answering this question, the study seeks to inform contemporary debates about the future of cash bail, the design of pretrial risk assessments, and the development of fairer and more accurate frameworks for pretrial decision-making in the United States.

Chapter 2:

Foundations of Bail in the U.S.

Pretrial detainees constitute the majority of individuals held in local jails in the United States. National data indicate that nearly two-thirds of those confined in jails are awaiting trial rather than serving a sentence following conviction (Digard & Swavola, 2019). This heavy reliance on pretrial detention both reflects and reinforces broader inequalities within the criminal justice system, particularly along lines of race and class. For example, in 2002, approximately 69% of pretrial detainees were people of color, despite representing a substantially smaller share of the overall U.S. population (Sawyer, 2019). Such disparities underscore persistent concerns that the bail system imposes its greatest burdens on low-income individuals and racial and ethnic minorities.

A large and growing body of research critiques the U.S. bail system for systematically penalizing defendants who lack the financial resources to secure release (D'Alessio & Stolzenberg, 2021). Because monetary bail functions as the primary gateway to pretrial freedom, many defendants remain incarcerated not because they pose heightened risks of flight or reoffending, but because they are unable to afford release. More than 60% of arrested individuals are detained pretrial solely because they are unable to post bond (Donnelly & MacDonald, 2018). The consequences are substantial: presumed-innocent defendants frequently experience job loss, housing instability, family disruption, and diminished capacity to assist in their own defense.

Nearly all jurisdictions in the United States rely on bond schedules— preset monetary amounts tied to specific offenses—to determine bail at or shortly after arrest. Designed to promote administrative efficiency in high-volume court systems, these schedules typically increase bail amounts based on the statutory seriousness of the offense. While they may expedite case processing, bond schedules have been widely criticized for embedding structural inequities into the release process. Because they rarely account for a defendant's financial circumstances or individualized risk, they operate as fixed-price mechanisms that disproportionately burden economically disadvantaged defendants, including those accused of relatively minor offenses (Dobbie et al., 2018).

Scholars have also challenged the assumption that monetary bail improves public safety. Holsinger and Holsinger (2018) argue that the ability to pay bail is only weakly related to the likelihood of reoffending. Wealthier defendants who may pose substantial risks can often secure release, while indigent defendants who pose minimal risk remain confined. This inversion of risk and liberty undermines the normative and practical justifications for financial bail, revealing a system in which economic status frequently outweighs public safety considerations in pretrial detention decisions.

An expanding empirical literature further suggests that a defendant's prior criminal history—largely absent from most bond schedules—is a substantially stronger predictor of pretrial failure than the severity of the current charge alone. D'Alessio and Stolzenberg (2021) demonstrate that prior convictions are strongly associated with pretrial rearrest, indicating that incorporating criminal history into pretrial decision-making may better promote public safety than reliance on offense seriousness as the primary determinant of bail. These findings cast serious doubt on the predictive validity of conventional charge-based bond schedules.

Taken together, this evidence reflects a growing consensus among scholars, practitioners, and reformers: the contemporary bail system disproportionately harms economically disadvantaged defendants, inadequately captures genuine risk, and relies on practices increasingly misaligned with empirical evidence. These shortcomings have fueled ongoing reform efforts to constrain the routine use of monetary bail, expand pretrial services, and shift toward more equitable and empirically grounded frameworks for pretrial release.

Legal Challenges of Bail Schedules

The constitutionality of bail schedules has come under increasing scrutiny in recent years. Proponents contend that schedules facilitate the rapid release of arrestees (Allen, 2016) and enable courts to manage heavy caseloads efficiently (Hurley, 2016). Critics counter that these administrative benefits are achieved at the expense of individualized justice. By assigning standardized bail amounts primarily based on the charged offense, bail schedules often disregard defendants' personal circumstances, particularly their financial capacity to secure release.

This tension between administrative efficiency and individualized assessment raises significant constitutional concerns, particularly in light of the Supreme Court's decision in Stack v. Boyle (1951). In Stack, the Court held that bail must be based on factors relevant to ensuring the defendant's appearance, not on broad generalizations tied solely to the offense charged. In a footnote referencing the Federal Rules of Criminal Procedure, the Court further indicated that bail determinations must consider a defendant's financial resources, among other personal characteristics. Although Stack established that uniform bail practices that ignore individual circumstances may violate the Eighth Amendment's prohibition on excessive bail, it left unresolved the precise boundaries of what constitutes "reasonable" bail, granting lower courts considerable interpretive discretion.

Empirical research suggests that contemporary bail practices often depart substantially from these constitutional principles. In a qualitative study of two California counties, Ottone and Scott-Hayward (2018) found that bail schedules emphasizing offense severity largely dictated release decisions, with minimal attention to defendants' economic circumstances. Their findings highlight a persistent gap between the individualized, proportional standard articulated in Stack and the routine reliance on rigid, offense-based schedules in everyday court operations.

Challenges to fixed bail systems have also arisen under the Fourteenth Amendment's Due Process and Equal Protection Clauses. Because indigent defendants remain detained while wealthier individuals facing similar charges secure release, courts increasingly recognize that wealth-based detention constitutes a deprivation of liberty that implicates both fairness and equality. As Allen (2016) observes, detaining individuals solely because of poverty transforms monetary bail into a mechanism of pretrial punishment and undermines the presumption of innocence.

A leading example of such litigation is O'Donnell v. Harris County, Texas (2018), a class action lawsuit challenging the county's misdemeanor bail practices. Plaintiffs argued that the county's use of a fixed money bail schedule violated the Due Process and Equal Protection Clauses by detaining indigent defendants without meaningful consideration of their ability to pay. The Fifth Circuit concluded that the system produced unconstitutional wealth-based detention, and the resulting consent decree mandated individualized assessments of financial capacity and periodic judicial review of detention decisions.

In several additional federal cases, the U.S. Department of Justice has filed Statements of Interest asserting that detaining individuals before trial solely because they cannot afford bail violates the Equal Protection Clause by treating indigent defendants differently from similarly situated defendants with greater financial resources (Heaton et al., 2017). These interventions signal a growing national recognition that bail schedules, when enforced without individualized review, function as arbitrary, wealth-based barriers to pretrial liberty.

Scholars have questioned whether litigation alone can fundamentally transform entrenched bail practices. Calaway and Kinsley (2018) argue that although constitutional challenges have generated important rulings against rigid bail schedules, institutional inertia, local political pressures, and resource constraints limit the transformative reach of court decisions in the absence of complementary legislative reform. Murtha (2024), after examining multiple cases from the Eastern District, reaches a similar conclusion: despite increasing judicial requirements to consider defendants' financial capacity, widespread reliance on bail schedules persists.

Taken together, this body of case law and scholarship demonstrates that bail schedules continue to drive arbitrary, wealth-based detention in many jurisdictions. Even where courts have acknowledged their constitutional deficiencies, these practices remain deeply embedded in routine court operations. The result is ongoing and unnecessary pretrial incarceration for indigent defendants, with significant consequences for case outcomes, future offending, and the perceived legitimacy of the criminal legal system.

Consequences of Pretrial Detention

Conviction

A substantial body of research demonstrates that pretrial detention significantly increases the likelihood of conviction (Dobbie et al., 2018). A central reason is that confinement itself exerts powerful pressure on defendants to resolve their cases quickly, often through guilty pleas, in order to secure release or improve living conditions (Lerman et al., 2022). Although both jails and prisons are custodial institutions, pretrial confinement in jails differs in important ways. Jail stays are typically shorter, but they are characterized by heightened uncertainty, fewer rehabilitative resources, rapid population turnover, and unstable conditions that can intensify psychological stress and constrain defendants' ability to participate effectively in their own defense (Turney, 2021).

Local jails generally lack the programming and rehabilitative services more commonly found, though still unevenly delivered, in prisons (Wildeman et al., 2018). Overcrowding is persistent, as jails must absorb continuous inflows of new arrestees and individuals serving short sentences. High turnover and limited space generate tension, strain safety, and degrade living conditions (Cornelius, 2012). Visitation is also more restricted in jails than in most prisons. Contact with family often occurs through plexiglass barriers, under tight time constraints, and with limited privacy, in contrast to many prison settings, where longer visits, shared meals, and more interactive environments are sometimes available (Turney, 2021).

Resource constraints further distinguish jails from prisons. Chronic underfunding and rapid population turnover hinder the delivery of adequate medical, mental health, and educational services (Schnittker et al., 2011). As a result, detainees face significant barriers to receiving necessary care and support, which can compound preexisting vulnerabilities and undermine future reintegration.

Mental health presents an especially acute concern. Jails are often ill-equipped to provide consistent mental health treatment, and short stays make continuity of care difficult (Steadman et al., 2009). Limited access to clinicians, medications, and therapeutic interventions contributes to untreated or poorly managed mental health conditions. These deficiencies are reflected in elevated rates of self-harm and suicide; jails exhibit persistently high suicide rates relative to other custodial settings (Fazel & Baillargeon, 2011).

In this environment, pretrial detainees face powerful incentives to plead guilty, even when viable defenses exist. In many jurisdictions, defendants may wait weeks or months before receiving appointed counsel or appearing for arraignment. Stevenson (2018) observes that in some jurisdictions "arraignments do not happen until six months after the bail hearing," leaving defendants who cannot secure release confined for prolonged periods before entering a plea (p. 6). Decades earlier, during the signing of the Bail Reform Act of

1966, President Lyndon B. Johnson similarly acknowledged that poor defendants often remained in jail "for weeks, months, and perhaps even years before trial" (Carlucci, 2019, p. 1207).

Pretrial detainees frequently plead guilty to escape adverse confinement conditions, protect employment and housing, retain custody of children, or obtain credit for time served (Sandberg, 2023). Confinement also restricts their ability to meet with attorneys, gather evidence, and otherwise participate in building a defense (Digard & Swavola, 2019).

Empirical evidence confirms these dynamics. Leslie and Pope (2017), analyzing more than one million felony and misdemeanor cases in New York between 2009 and 2013, found that among defendants unable to post bail, pretrial detention increased the probability of conviction for felony defendants by approximately 13% and increased the likelihood of pleading guilty by roughly 10%. In the misdemeanor sample, more than half of detained defendants faced bail below $2,000, illustrating how even relatively modest amounts can be prohibitive for individuals with limited financial resources.

Petersen (2020), using data from large urban counties between 1990 and 2004, reported that detained defendants pled guilty 2.86 times faster than released defendants. Petersen concluded that overcrowding, harsh living conditions, uncertainty about case duration, financial strain, and concern for family obligations jointly contributed to earlier and more frequent guilty pleas among detainees.

Using a judge-fixed-effects instrumental variables strategy, Koppel et al. (2022) found that pretrial detention increased the likelihood of pleading guilty by 23%, the likelihood of conviction by 24%, and the likelihood of receiving a custodial sentence by 35%. Notably, 98% of these convictions resulted from guilty pleas rather than trials, underscoring the coercive influence of pretrial detention on case outcomes.

Sentencing Decisions

Pretrial detention also exerts a substantial and independent influence on sentencing outcomes. A large body of research demonstrates that defendants detained prior to trial are significantly more likely to receive custodial sentences and longer incarceration terms than similarly situated defendants released (Digard & Swavola, 2019). Early scholarship recognized this relationship, linking pretrial detention to elevated incarceration rates at sentencing (Goldkamp, 1980).

More recent studies have documented the magnitude of these effects on sentence severity. Stevenson (2018), examining 331,971 cases in Philadelphia between 2006 and 2013, found that pretrial detention increased the eventual length of incarceration by approximately 42%. When disaggregating by offense type, the effects were particularly pronounced among misdemeanor defendants, who experienced substantial increases in adverse prosecutorial and sentencing outcomes.

Lowenkamp et al. (2013), analyzing 153,407 defendants in Kentucky between July 2009 and June 2010, concluded that individuals detained throughout the pretrial period were 4.44 times as likely to receive a jail sentence and 3.32 times as likely to receive a prison sentence as defendants who secured release at any point before case disposition. They further found that defendants detained for the entire pretrial period received significantly longer sentences than their released counterparts.

Notably, several studies indicate that the most damaging sentencing consequences of pretrial detention are borne by defendants assessed as low risk (Digard & Swavola, 2019). Lowenkamp et al. (2013) reported that low-risk defendants detained throughout the pretrial period were 5.41 times as likely to receive a jail sentence and 3.76 times as likely to receive a prison sentence as comparable low-risk defendants released before trial. Stevenson (2018) similarly found that among misdemeanor cases, pretrial detention increased the probability of receiving a custodial sentence by 7.6% relative to a baseline incarceration rate of 16%. Detained defendants were also substantially more likely to receive "time served" sentences, effectively converting pretrial detention itself into the primary form of punishment.

Impact of Pretrial Detention on Future Arrests and Failures to Appear

Although pretrial detention is often justified because it temporarily incapacitates defendants and thereby reduces crime, empirical research suggests that detention may, in fact, increase both future criminal behavior and failures to appear after case disposition (Dobbie et al., 2018). Rather than functioning as a durable crime-control strategy, pretrial detention appears to generate destabilizing effects that elevate subsequent risk across multiple dimensions of pretrial failure.

Leslie and Pope (2017) found that pretrial detention was associated with higher rates of recidivism among both felony and misdemeanor defendants. For felony defendants, pretrial detention increased the probability of conviction by 13% and was accompanied by a 7.5% increase in the likelihood of rearrest within two years of case disposition. They also documented elevated rates of missed court appearances among previously detained defendants, indicating that detention does not reliably promote long-term court compliance.

Lowenkamp et al. (2013) reported similar findings. Defendants detained throughout the pretrial period were 1.3 times as likely to be rearrested after case disposition as those released at any point prior to trial, even when detention lasted as little as 2 days. Notably, the same group also exhibited higher rates of failure to appear following release, further undermining the assumption that pretrial detention produces lasting compliance with court obligations.

Several mechanisms help explain these patterns. Pretrial detention disrupts employment and income, weakening economic stability and increasing financial strain (Dobbie et al., 2018). It also strains family relationships and erodes community ties—key protective factors that support both lawful behavior and court compliance (Heaton et al., 2017). By destabilizing the social and economic foundations of defendants' lives, pretrial detention may unintentionally increase the high risks it is intended to prevent.

Physical and Emotional Effects

The coercive power of pretrial confinement extends beyond the mere loss of liberty to encompass significant physical and psychological harms associated with jail conditions. Defendants who are unable to secure bail release routinely experience serious health and emotional consequences that shape both their immediate legal decision-making and their long-term well-being (Futrell, 2020).

Conditions of confinement—including overcrowding, unsanitary facilities, inadequate medical care, limited access to mental health services, and heightened exposure to violence—exert continuous pressure on detained individuals. These conditions become central to defendants' calculus when deciding whether to exercise their right to trial or accept a plea agreement, particularly when continued detention threatens physical safety, psychological stability, employment, housing, and family relationships.

By embedding such coercive pressures into the pretrial process, the current bail system transforms confinement itself into a powerful instrument of case resolution rather than a neutral mechanism for ensuring court appearance and public safety.

Sexual Assault

Sexual victimization is a pervasive and serious problem in correctional institutions. In 2018, more than 27,000 allegations of sexual abuse were reported in prisons, jails, and other adult correctional settings (Buehler, 2021). Reported allegations increased by approximately 180% between 2011 and 2015, reflecting both heightened awareness and persistent institutional failures to prevent abuse. Although early research focused primarily on male victimization, subsequent studies demonstrate that women are also at substantial risk and, in some contexts, report higher rates of sexual victimization than men (Caravaca-Sánchez & Wolff, 2016). Struckman-Johnson et al. (1996) found that 7% of incarcerated women and 22% of incarcerated men reported experiencing sexual violence, while later research indicates rising rates of victimization among women (Struckman-Johnson & Struckman-Johnson, 2002).

Sexual abuse is not limited to violence between incarcerated individuals; sexual victimization by correctional staff also constitutes a significant portion of reported cases. Data from the National Inmate Survey indicate that approximately 2% of jail inmates report sexual contact with staff, with much of this occurring during the initial months of incarceration (Beck et al., 2013). Pretrial detainees—newly confined, disoriented, and often unfamiliar with jail environments—may be particularly vulnerable to such abuse. The heightened exposure to victimization during early confinement further illustrates the profound risks imposed by pretrial detention and the coercive pressures shaping defendants' legal decision-making.

Suicide

Suicide and self-harm represent some of the most severe health risks in local jails. Between 2000 and 2014, suicide was the leading cause of death in U.S. jails, accounting for approximately 25 to 35% of all jail deaths (Metzner & Hayes, 2020). In prisons, by contrast, suicide ranked as the fourth leading cause of death, behind cancer, heart disease, and liver disease. The timing of suicide in jail is especially critical: roughly 23% of jail suicides occur within the first 24 hours of confinement, when individuals experience acute psychological shock, withdrawal, and extreme stress.

Self-harm is likewise alarmingly prevalent and constitutes a major source of morbidity in correctional environments (Favril et al., 2020). Individuals who engage in self-harm while incarcerated face a six- to eight-fold increased risk of suicide during confinement and remain at elevated risk after release (Winicov, 2019). Pretrial detainees are particularly vulnerable, as they often confront profound uncertainty regarding their legal fate while being abruptly severed from family, employment, and community supports.

Together, these patterns illustrate how the conditions and timing of pretrial detention can produce acute psychological crises with life-threatening consequences, further underscoring the human costs embedded within contemporary bail practices.

COVID-19

The COVID-19 pandemic sharply intensified longstanding health and safety concerns within jails and prisons. In 2020, the World Health Organization (WHO) declared COVID-19 a global public health emergency, emphasizing that the virus spreads most efficiently in crowded, close-contact, and poorly ventilated indoor environments—the "Three Cs" (World Health Organization, 2021). Correctional facilities exemplify each of these risk factors. Chronic overcrowding, limited capacity for physical distancing, and institutional priorities that privilege security over health made viral containment especially difficult (Wang et al., 2021).

Jail populations declined by approximately 24% during the first half of 2020 as jurisdictions implemented emergency decarceration measures to slow the transmission of COVID-19 (Washington, 2021). Nevertheless, many individuals remained confined under conditions that further impaired physical and psychological well-being while severing connections to family and community (Charles et al., 2022). Visitation was suspended or sharply curtailed, symptomatic individuals were placed in medical isolation or solitary confinement, and many facilities imposed prolonged lockdowns, mandatory testing, and severe restrictions on movement. Although some jails provided free video calls, others did not, exacerbating financial and emotional strain—particularly for low-income families (Charles et al., 2022).

The health risks associated with incarceration long predated the pandemic. Infection rates for communicable diseases such as hepatitis C (Boutwell et al., 2005), HIV/AIDS (Rowell-Cunsolo et al., 2016), and other sexually transmitted infections (Hammett, 2009) have historically exceeded those of the general population. Structural conditions—including overcrowding, poor sanitation, aging infrastructure, and inconsistent access to medical care— amplify these risks. In some cases, failures of care within correctional facilities have reached the level of "deliberate indifference to serious medical needs" (Uggen et al., 2023, p. 2).

During the pandemic, correctional systems implemented testing and vaccination programs, yet infection rates among incarcerated populations remained substantially higher than in the community (Puglisi et al., 2023). Early in the pandemic, incarcerated individuals were infected at more than four times the rate of non-incarcerated persons (Schwartzapfel et al., 2020). Deep distrust of correctional health systems—where care frequently falls below community standards—discouraged some detainees from seeking treatment, further compounding risk (Kincaid, 2023).

Qualitative research on lived experience during COVID-19 underscores these harms. Charles et al. (2022), in interviews with 33 individuals detained in a mid-sized county jail—predominantly Black men, many of them parents—documented severe adverse effects on mental health, family relationships, and daily life. Participants described profound isolation, persistent fear of infection, and emotional strain intensified by the loss of visitation and community contact.

Recent data indicate that pandemic-related population reductions were temporary. Although admissions declined in 2020 and 2021 due to reduced reported crime, suspended transfers, and delayed court operations, jail populations have since rebounded as courts resumed normal functioning (Sawyer & Wagner, 2023). Racial disparities remain pronounced: even amid population declines between 2019 and 2020, Black individuals were incarcerated at 3.5 times the rate of White individuals (Puglisi et al., 2023).

Employment Implications

Pretrial detention carries profound consequences for employment and economic stability. Defendants who are unable to secure bail release frequently lose their jobs, triggering immediate financial strain that affects both their personal lives and the course of their legal cases. Job loss undermines the ability to pay legal fees, fines, and court costs, and it diminishes prospects for stable reentry following release.

Incarceration also disrupts access to social services, job training, and educational programs that could otherwise support employment, particularly for individuals with limited work histories or lower educational attainment (Hagan, 1993). These economic disruptions are not evenly distributed. The financial toll of incarceration is especially severe for racial and ethnic minorities. Western (2006) estimates that incarceration reduces lifetime earnings by approximately 1% for White men, 2% for Hispanic men, and 4% for Black men. Pettit and Lyons (2007) further find that although earnings eventually recover, Black men take significantly longer than their White and Hispanic counterparts to return to pre-incarceration income levels. Persistent discrimination against individuals with criminal records intensifies these disparities (Agan & Starr, 2018). As one study concluded, for Black men "nothing created as great a stigma…as the possession of a criminal record" (Young, 2003, p. 232).

Empirical evidence specifically linking pretrial detention to employment loss reinforces these conclusions. Dobbie et al. (2018) examined pretrial detention in Miami-Dade County, where a charge-based bail schedule is used. Defendants unable to post scheduled bail within 24 hours appeared before a judge, who could modify the amount, though such adjustments were relatively rare. The authors found that pretrial detention significantly reduced employment prospects for three to four years following the bail hearing. In related work, Dobbie and Yang (2021) reported that detention increased reliance on unemployment insurance and reduced take-up of the Earned Income Tax Credit (EITC). They attribute these outcomes to the stigmatizing effects of criminal records and the disruption of employment trajectories caused by arrest and detention.

Criminal records also generate substantial barriers at the point of hire. Pager's (2003) audit study revealed that job applicants with documented prison sentences received callback rates approximately 50% lower than otherwise similar applicants without records. Although some administrative studies observe modest short-term increases in employment following release (LaLonde & Cho, 2008), these gains are often temporary and fail to offset the broader economic harms associated with criminal justice involvement. Legal financial obligations further compound disadvantage by reducing family income, restricting access to housing, credit, transportation, and employment, and increasing the likelihood of continued contact with the criminal justice system (Harris et al., 2010).

Stigma of Criminalization

The consequences of pretrial detention extend well beyond direct financial loss to include profound and enduring forms of social stigma. Involvement in the criminal justice system can isolate individuals—especially youth—from their communities, schools, and support networks, weakening social bonds and disrupting normal developmental trajectories (Conklln, 2011). Defendants frequently experience what Pager (2008) describes as "psychic costs" associated with being labeled as a criminal, which can lead to defensive behavior, strained interpersonal relationships, and diminished self-concept. Stigma also damages civic reputation (Lessnick, 2022) and generates professional pressures, including for defense attorneys whose own reputations may be affected by case outcomes (Klein, 1997).

Empirical research demonstrates how quickly these effects emerge. Holsinger and Holsinger (2018) found that defendants detained pretrial for as little as three days faced a 76% probability of employment disruption and a 37% probability of residential instability, financial distress, and strained relationships with dependent children. These disruptions frequently cascade, producing long-term consequences even for individuals who are ultimately acquitted or receive noncustodial sentences.

Court obligations further intensify stigma and strain. Hearings are commonly scheduled during working hours, and court dockets are routinely overbooked, resulting in defendants waiting for extended periods—sometimes hours or even days—for brief appearances. The repeated need to miss work, arrange childcare, and manage transportation imposes substantial burdens. Many defendants attempt to conceal their involvement in the criminal process from employers, educators, childcare providers, and family members, thereby amplifying stress, social isolation, and stigma (Carroll, 2021).

Disparities in Pretrial Detention and Sentencing

The pretrial phase of criminal processing exhibits pronounced racial and ethnic disparities that both reflect and reinforce structural inequalities within the broader criminal legal system. A large body of research demonstrates that racial and ethnic minorities— particularly Black and Latino defendants—are detained more frequently, subjected to more restrictive bail conditions, and less likely to secure release than similarly situated White defendants (Barno et al., 2020).

Early work documented the role of socioeconomic status in shaping these outcomes. Albonetti (1989) found that White defendants with higher levels of education and income were significantly less likely to be detained. In contrast, Lynch and Patterson (1991) reported that non-White defendants were less likely than White defendants to receive bail amounts below guideline recommendations. Similarly, Nagel (1982), analyzing data from a New York City borough in the mid-1970s, found that White defendants were more likely to receive lower bail amounts and to be offered cash alternatives to surety bonds, although these advantages did not always translate into higher rates of nonfinancial release.

Subsequent research confirmed that race continues to shape pretrial outcomes even after accounting for legal factors. Katz and Spohn (1995), studying defendants charged with violent felonies in Detroit, found that race and gender influenced the likelihood of pretrial incarceration. Although they identified gender disparities in bail amounts and did not observe statistically significant racial differences in bail levels, Black defendants remained less likely to be released and more likely to experience pretrial incarceration. Demuth (2003), examining felony defendants in large urban counties, identified racial and ethnic disparities at multiple stages of pretrial processing, with Latino defendants often facing harsher treatment than Black defendants. Both Katz and Spohn (1995) and Demuth (2003) concluded that Black defendants were less likely to be released, less likely to make bail, and more likely to be denied bail than White defendants.

These disparities extend directly into sentencing outcomes. Demuth (2003) found that race and ethnicity significantly influenced bail-denial decisions, which, in turn, shaped subsequent case trajectories. Demuth and Steffensmeier (2004) reported that Hispanic and Black defendants were significantly more likely to be denied bail than White defendants, while gender played a comparatively minor role. Schlesinger (2005) similarly found that Black and Hispanic defendants were approximately 25% more likely than White defendants to be denied bail, with some estimates indicating that Hispanic defendants were 67% more likely and Black defendants 80% more likely to be denied bail when controlling for legally relevant factors.

Collectively, this literature demonstrates that racial and ethnic inequality is deeply embedded within pretrial decision-making and that these disparities reverberate through subsequent sentencing outcomes. Pretrial detention thus functions not only as a mechanism of case processing but also as a powerful driver of cumulative disadvantage across the criminal justice system.

Bail Reforms and Alternatives

The research reviewed above underscores the urgent need for meaningful bail reform. Contemporary reform efforts generally seek to reduce reliance on monetary bail, address racial and socioeconomic disparities in pretrial detention, improve the quality and fairness of bail hearings, and incorporate actuarial risk assessment tools to inform release decisions better (D'Alessio & Stolzenberg, 2021).

Meaningful Bail Hearings

One central reform strategy is the promotion of "meaningful" bail hearings—proceedings that genuinely consider a defendant's individual circumstances, including financial capacity, community ties, and risk (Digard & Swavola, 2019). In practice, bail hearings frequently occur within 24 to 48 hours of arrest and often last only a few minutes, limiting judges' ability to gather and assess relevant information (Dobbie et al., 2018). Some scholars argue that modest delays could allow courts to obtain more complete information and improve the accuracy of release decisions (Stevenson & Mayson, 2017). At the same time, delayed hearings necessarily extend initial detention, underscoring the importance of balancing procedural thoroughness against the harms of continued confinement.

Assistance of Defense Counsel

Another critical reform involves ensuring the presence of defense counsel at bail hearings. Although the Sixth Amendment guarantees the right to counsel and Gideon v. Wainwright (1963) requires states to provide attorneys to indigent defendants, this protection applies only to proceedings deemed "critical stages" of the criminal process

(Stevenson & Mayson, 2017). In many jurisdictions, bail hearings are not classified as such, leaving defendants to appear without representation (Anwar et al., 2023).

Empirical evidence demonstrates the importance of counsel at this early stage. The Lawyers at Bail (LAB) Project in Baltimore conducted a randomized experiment in 1998 that provided attorneys to 57% of a sample of 300 low-income, nonviolent defendants at their bail or bail-review hearings, while the remaining 43% appeared without representation (Colbert et al., 2002). Defendants with counsel were significantly more likely to be released on recognizance, to receive lower bail amounts, and to spend fewer days in jail. These results indicate that early legal representation can substantially reduce unnecessary detention and produce cost savings for court systems.

More recently, Anwar et al. (2023) evaluated a year-long initiative in Allegheny County, Pennsylvania, that provided public defenders at bail hearings. The presence of counsel reduced the use of monetary bail and pretrial detention by 21% without increasing failure-to-appear rates or negatively affecting probable-cause determinations. These findings suggest that representation at the bail stage can promote both liberty and fairness without compromising court appearance or public safety.

Defense counsel plays a vital role by presenting information about defendants' community ties, employment, caregiving responsibilities, and financial circumstances, and by advocating for nonmonetary conditions of release (Anwar et al., 2023). However, Anwar et al. (2023) also documented a short-term increase in rearrests for third-degree felony theft within six months of the bail hearing. They therefore recommend careful cost–benefit analyses that weigh the harms of detention against the social costs of additional property offenses—an approach that reflects the broader tradeoffs inherent in pretrial reform.

Court Date Reminders, Pretrial Supervision, and Unsecured Bonds

Another set of reform strategies focuses on reducing failure to appear (FTA) through low-cost procedural innovations and alternatives to monetary bail. A substantial proportion of FTAs result from defendants forgetting court dates, misplacing paperwork, or encountering routine logistical obstacles (Zottola et al., 2023a). Empirical studies indicate that simple reminder systems—delivered through phone calls, text messages, or mailed notices—can meaningfully improve court appearance rates (Fishbane et al., 2020). Schnacke et al. (2012) reported that telephone reminders increased appearance rates by up to 42%, whereas mailed reminders increased appearance rates by up to 33%. In Lafayette Parish, Louisiana, Howat et al. (2016) documented an increase in overall appearance rates from 48% to 62% following the introduction of telephone reminder calls.

The broader evidence, however, suggests more modest effects. Zottola et al. (2023a), in a systematic review and meta-analysis of twelve reminder studies conducted between 1977 and 2019, concluded that reminders produced statistically significant but generally limited reductions in FTA. Hatton and Smith (2020) likewise observed significant improvements in court appearance in Louisiana, Nebraska, New York, and Oregon, but not in Kentucky. These findings indicate that reminders are helpful but insufficient as a stand-alone reform.

Many jurisdictions have also expanded the use of unsecured bonds and non-monetary conditions of release. Under unsecured bonds, defendants do not pay money up front but agree to become financially liable if they fail to appear (Ouss & Stevenson, 2023). Jones (2013), analyzing 1,970 defendants in ten Colorado jails, found that unsecured bonds were as effective as secured bonds in ensuring court appearance and maintaining public safety. Other scholars have recommended deposit or partially secured bonds, in which funds are returned upon compliance with court conditions (Digard & Swavola, 2019).

Nonfinancial conditions of release—including pretrial supervision, regular check-ins, drug testing, and electronic monitoring—are now widely used (Hatton & Smith, 2020). The evidence regarding their effectiveness, however, remains mixed. Hatton and Smith (2020), reviewing Washington, D.C.'s NIJ-funded pretrial initiatives and comparable programs, identified only two studies demonstrating significant reductions in either FTAs or rearrests: one in Washington, D.C., and another in Pima County, Arizona.

Research on substance use treatment as a pretrial condition is similarly inconclusive. Kopak and Singer (2023) found that defendants with certain substance use disorders were four times more likely to experience adverse outcomes associated with FTA, highlighting the need for more targeted research on how treatment conditions interact with pretrial compliance.

Electronic monitoring (EM) has expanded substantially since the enactment of the Bail Reform Act of 1984. EM devices—typically ankle-mounted—allow authorities to track defendants' movements and enforce curfews or geographic restrictions (Cherson, 2022a). Despite widespread adoption, evidence of EM's effectiveness remains limited and inconsistent (Smith & Robson, 2022). Some studies report modest reductions in either FTAs or rearrests, but rarely both, and note increased rates of technical violations (Hatton & Smith, 2020). EM has also been criticized for imposing additional financial burdens through supervision fees and for disproportionately affecting Black and low-income defendants (Cherson, 2022a). Documented harms include job loss, reduced employment opportunities, strained family relationships, psychological distress, and physical discomfort or injury from monitoring devices (Cherson, 2022a).

Pretrial supervision programs more broadly yield uneven results. Hatton and Smith (2020), in a review of eight studies, found that only half reported statistically significant reductions in FTAs among supervised defendants. Lowenkamp and Bechtel (2009), using the Virginia Pretrial Risk Assessment Instrument (VPRAI) in Summit County, Ohio, similarly concluded that supervision did not significantly reduce FTAs among low-risk defendants.

More promising results emerge when supervision is tightly targeted using validated risk tools. Barno et al. (2020) found that defendants supervised through Orange County, California's Pretrial Assessment and Release Supervision (PARS) program—where supervision intensity was matched to VPRAI risk levels—had 43% lower odds of FTA than similarly situated defendants released on monetary bail. These findings suggest that carefully targeted, risk-informed supervision can improve court appearance while reducing reliance on financial bail.

Risk Assessment Instruments

The findings of Lowenkamp and Bechtel (2009) and Barno et al. (2020) underscore the potential of pretrial risk assessment instruments to predict both failure to appear (FTA) and new criminal activity. These tools employ statistical models to estimate the likelihood that a defendant will fail to appear in court or be rearrested during the pretrial period based on factors such as criminal history, current charges, and indicators of social stability or instability (Cherson, 2022b). Defendants are then classified into risk categories that are intended to guide judicial decisions regarding release conditions (Desmarais & Lowder, 2019).

One of the most extensively studied instruments is the Virginia Pretrial Risk Assessment Instrument (VPRAI). Using multivariate logistic regression, Lowenkamp and Bechtel (2009) found that most VPRAI factors significantly predicted FTAs. They further identified three variables—pending charges, two or more prior violent convictions, and employment or primary caregiver status—that predicted both FTAs and rearrests.

Another widely adopted instrument is the Public Safety Assessment (PSA), developed by the Laura and John Arnold Foundation. Created through a two-year research initiative, the PSA uses nine factors—age at arrest, current violent offense, pending charges, prior misdemeanor convictions, prior felony convictions, prior violent convictions, prior FTAs within two years, prior FTAs beyond two years, and prior sentences to incarceration—to estimate the risk of new criminal activity, new violent offending, and failure to appear (Kennedy et al., 2013).

Empirical evaluations suggest that these tools can meaningfully influence pretrial outcomes. Brooker (2017), comparing pre- and post-implementation periods in a single jurisdiction, found that PSA-based reforms increased pretrial release rates without significantly affecting FTA or new arrest rates. Redcross et al. (2019) similarly reported that after PSA implementation, more defendants were released, court appearance rates remained above 80%, and pretrial arrest rates remained stable. Lowder et al. (2021), evaluating the Indiana Risk Assessment System–Pretrial Assessment Tool (IRAS-PAT), found that jurisdictions using the instrument imposed fewer financial release conditions and increased overall pretrial release rates.

Proponents argue that risk assessment tools can reduce reliance on money bail and introduce more objective, evidence-based guidance into judicial decision-making (Copp et al., 2022). However, their real-world impact depends critically on how judges interpret and apply risk scores. Judges retain broad discretion to assign weight to risk assessments and to depart from tool recommendations (Barno et al., 2020).

Critics caution that these instruments may entrench racial disparities because they rely on data—such as prior arrests, convictions, and neighborhood characteristics—that are themselves shaped by structural inequality and biased enforcement practices (Cherson, 2022b). Research further indicates that judges frequently override tool recommendations, particularly when the tool suggests release (Copp et al., 2022). Zottola et al. (2023b), in an online survey of 246 pretrial decision-makers, found that at high risk levels, Black defendants were more likely than White defendants to be recommended for release with conditions, suggesting complex interactions between race, perceived risk, and judicial responses to risk information. Copp et al. (2022), using multinomial logistic regression, likewise found that judges in one jurisdiction disregarded release-on-recognizance recommendations nearly half the time and were more likely to impose financial conditions even when supervised release was recommended. They also documented higher rates of departure from release recommendations for Black and Latino defendants than for White defendants.

Some scholars further argue that risk assessment tools generate more "false positives" than "false negatives," meaning that individuals predicted to fail often comply with conditions, whereas those predicted to succeed rarely receive that classification (Cherson, 2022b). Fear of public backlash when a released defendant commits a serious offense may lead judges to override low-risk recommendations despite favorable risk scores (Moore, 2022).

In sum, risk assessment instruments represent an important component of modern bail reform, with the potential to reduce unnecessary detention and reliance on monetary bail. Their effectiveness, however, depends on the integrity of their design, the fairness of the data on which they rely, the consistency of judicial application, and the broader legal and political environment in which they operate. Risk assessment tools are, therefore, not a cure-all, but rather one element within a broader strategy for building a more equitable, evidence-based, and constitutionally grounded system of pretrial justice.

Chapter 3:

Theoretical Framework

This study is guided by labeling theory as its primary theoretical framework. Although a substantial empirical literature examines bail practices and pretrial release, relatively few studies explicitly address *why* individuals with prior criminal records are more likely to experience pretrial failure. Several established theoretical perspectives speak to compliance and offending under legal supervision, including procedural justice (Tyler, 2003), self-control theory (Gottfredson & Hirschi, 1990), general strain theory (Agnew, 2017), social bond theory (Hirschi, 1969), and defiance theory (Sherman, 1993). Each offers important insight into behavior, perceived legitimacy, and compliance in the context of legal authority. Yet, as Stolzenberg et al. (2021) observe, the literature lacks a clear, unified framework that explains the specific role of prior criminal record in shaping pretrial rearrest and failure.

Labeling theory provides a particularly well-suited foundation for this analysis. Long recognized as a core perspective in the study of deviance and criminal careers, labeling theory emphasizes the consequences of formal social reactions to wrongdoing. Because the present study examines how defendants' prior criminal histories—measured by the number of convictions and arrests—affect the probability of pretrial failure, labeling theory offers a compelling interpretive lens. Rather than focusing on the legal seriousness of the current charge, labeling theory emphasizes how prior contact with the criminal justice system and the formal designation of "criminal" reshape self-concept, constrain legitimate opportunities, alter social relationships, and ultimately increase the likelihood of continued offending during the pretrial period.

An Overview of Labeling Theory

Language is a powerful social force. The terms used to describe individuals influence not only how others perceive them but also how people understand themselves. Cooley's (1902) classic concept of the *looking-glass self* captures this process: individuals form self-images by imagining how they appear to others, how others judge them, and by experiencing corresponding self-feelings such as pride or shame. A criminal conviction—formally designating an individual as an "offender" or "felon"—thus represents far more than a legal classification; it constitutes a socially consequential label imbued with stigma (Warren, 2023).

Building on Cooley's insight, Mead (1934) developed symbolic interactionism, arguing that the self emerges through social interaction as individuals internalize the perspectives of their communities—what he termed the "generalized other." When communities define certain behaviors and individuals as "deviant," those labeled may come to view themselves through that lens. Labeling theory extends this logic by emphasizing that deviance is not an inherent property of an act, but rather a social construction produced through collective reactions and official definitions (Becker, 1963).

Within criminology, Frank Tannenbaum is widely credited with the first explicit articulation of labeling processes in his concept of the "dramatization of evil" (Barmaki, 2019). Tannenbaum argued that the arrest of a youth initiates a sequence of experiences—public shaming, segregation, and formal processing—that reorganize the individual's identity:

The process of making the criminal, therefore, is a process of tagging, defining, identifying, segregating, describing, emphasizing, making conscious and self-conscious; it becomes a way of stimulating, suggesting, emphasizing, and evoking the very traits that are complained of.

(Tannenbaum, 1938, pp. 19–20)

From this perspective, the formal response to misconduct becomes "mischievous" precisely because it defines the individual as delinquent and, in doing so, amplifies the very behavior it seeks to suppress.

Lemert (1951) further advanced labeling theory by distinguishing between primary and secondary deviance. Primary deviance refers to initial rule violations that are often situational, episodic, and not incorporated into the individual's self-concept. Secondary deviance emerges when social reactions and labels are internalized, leading the individual to adopt a deviant identity and engage in behavior consistent with that role. Once publicly designated as criminal, individuals face constrained legitimate opportunities and increasing exposure to deviant networks, reinforcing continued involvement in deviance.

Howard Becker (1963) elaborated this framework in *Outsiders*, arguing that "social groups create deviance by making the rules whose infraction constitutes deviance and by applying those rules to particular people and labeling them as outsiders" (p. 9). For Becker, deviance results not simply from behavior, but from the application of rules and sanctions to particular actors. The deviant label reshapes how others respond to the individual and how the individual comes to understand themselves. Over time, labeled individuals may gravitate toward deviant subcultures in which their identity is validated, reinforced, and rewarded.

Taken together, labeling theory posits that formal contact with the criminal justice system—through arrest, conviction, and incarceration—along with the accompanying stigma, transforms both self-concept and social context in ways that heighten the risk of continued offending. This framework is especially relevant to pretrial contexts, where prior criminal record is both a powerful predictor of rearrest and a marker of accumulated stigma and structural disadvantage.

Labeling, Stigma, and Future Delinquent Behavior

In criminology, "labeling events" typically include police contact, arrest, conviction, and sentencing (Chiricos et al., 2007). These events carry social meanings that extend far beyond the courtroom. Individuals who are labeled frequently experience social exclusion, strained family relationships, employment barriers, and public distrust (Warren, 2023). Upon returning to the community, they encounter substantial structural obstacles, including limited educational opportunities, restricted access to employment, difficulty securing stable housing, transportation barriers, and ineligibility for many forms of financial assistance and public benefits (Warren, 2023).

Labeling theory predicts that these constraints can unintentionally promote continued involvement in crime. Excluded from conventional institutions and opportunities, individuals may seek acceptance and support within deviant peer networks where criminal behavior is normalized and sometimes valorized (Bernburg et al., 2006). Differential association theory offers a complementary explanation, emphasizing that exposure to delinquent peers increases the likelihood of internalizing definitions favorable to law violation (Sutherland, 1947). In practice, labeling processes and peer influence operate in mutually reinforcing ways.

Empirical research strongly supports this dynamic. Bernburg et al. (2006), using a longitudinal panel study of urban adolescents, found that official labeling through juvenile justice contact increased subsequent involvement in deviant peer networks, which in turn heightened the risk of later delinquency. Youth formally processed by the juvenile system were substantially more likely than their non-processed peers to join gangs and to engage in theft, vandalism, and violence. These findings demonstrate how official intervention can indirectly increase offending by reshaping social networks.

Hochstetler et al. (2002), analyzing data from the National Youth Survey, similarly reported that peers' attitudes and behaviors were strong predictors of individual offending across multiple crime types, including vandalism, theft, and assault. Their results align with differential association theory and reinforce labeling theory's emphasis on the social consequences of official contact.

More recently, Rowan et al. (2023) applied a labeling framework to examine whether formal processing influenced friendship selection among court-involved youth. In a sample of 1,216 racially diverse male adolescents under court supervision, formally processed youths had a 17% greater likelihood of forming new deviant peer ties over three years compared with those not formally processed. This evidence indicates that justice system involvement not only stigmatizes youth but also actively reshapes their social environments in ways that sustain delinquent behavior.

Motz et al. (2020), drawing on data from the Environmental Risk (E-Risk) Longitudinal Twin Study, provided further support for labeling effects. They examined self-reported delinquency at age 18, including fighting, bullying, cruelty, vandalism, theft, truancy, and running away—alongside various forms of justice system contact, such as spending a night in jail or prison, receiving an Anti-Social Behavior Order (ASBO), and obtaining an official criminal record. Individuals who experienced such contact were significantly more likely to engage in a wide range of delinquent behaviors, even after accounting for prior conduct.

Johnson et al. (2004), using longitudinal survey data spanning early adolescence through young adulthood, examined the interplay among prior criminal behavior, deviant peer associations, and justice system involvement. They found that system contact was consistently associated with future criminality at multiple developmental stages (grade 7, grade 10, and three years after high school). Although the relationship between deviant peers and later offending was more mixed in their analysis, the authors concluded that labeling theory is strengthened by a life-course perspective that recognizes how cumulative system contact and stigma shape criminal trajectories over time.

Collectively, this body of research underscores a central proposition of labeling theory: formal processing and criminal labeling reshape both self-identity and social environments in ways that elevate the risk of continued offending.

Public Stigmatization, Criminal Records, and Recidivism

A criminal record represents one of the most durable and visible forms of social stigma. Unlike many stigmatized statuses, it is typically permanent, easily reproduced through background checks, and legally consequential across multiple domains of life, including employment, housing, and civic participation (Chiricos et al., 2007). Even after individuals have formally "paid their debt" through incarceration, probation, or supervision, criminal records continue to constrain opportunities for full reintegration into society (Maruna, 2001).

Labeling theorists argue that this persistent stigma sustains a self-reinforcing cycle of disadvantage and recidivism. Barriers to legal employment, stable housing, access to credit, and civic inclusion restrict lawful opportunities and increase the likelihood of renewed criminal involvement when conventional pathways are blocked (Western, 2006). Unemployment, in particular, is a well-established predictor of recidivism (Kolbeck et al., 2022), and substantial evidence indicates that the formal label of "felon" significantly diminishes employment prospects (D'Alessio et al., 2014).

Empirical research supports these theoretical claims. D'Alessio et al. (2014) examined the effects of Hawaii's "Ban the Box" law, which prohibits employers from inquiring about criminal records until after a conditional job offer and limits the use of conviction information to the most recent ten years and to positions for which the conviction is directly relevant. Using longitudinal data from the State Court Processing Statistics (SCPS) program covering 1990–2004, they found that after the law's enactment in Honolulu, defendants accused of serious crimes exhibited a 57% lower probability of having a prior criminal conviction. The authors interpreted this decline as consistent with labeling theory: by delaying and restricting employer access to criminal record information, the policy appeared to reduce repeat offending.

Chiricos et al. (2007) conducted one of the first large-scale tests of labeling effects among adult offenders by examining how formal felony adjudication influences subsequent recidivism. In Florida, judges may withhold adjudication for some felony offenders sentenced to probation, thereby allowing them to avoid the official status of "convicted felon." Comparing individuals whose guilt was formally adjudicated with those who received a withhold, the authors found that a formal conviction significantly increased the likelihood of reconviction within two years. These findings provide strong empirical support for labeling theory's central claim that official criminal status, independent of underlying behavior, increases the risk of continued offending.

In sum, the criminal label operates not only through internalized identity change but also through enduring, externally imposed structural barriers that limit social and economic participation and perpetuate criminal involvement.

Implications of Labeling Theory for Bail and Pretrial Decisions

Labeling theory has direct and important implications for understanding pretrial outcomes and for evaluating contemporary bail practices. Prior research consistently shows that individuals with prior criminal histories are more likely to experience pretrial failure—through new offending or rearrest—than individuals without such histories (Gottfredson & Gottfredson, 1988). From a labeling perspective, this pattern does not simply reflect a stable underlying propensity for crime. Rather, it reflects the cumulative consequences of stigma, structural exclusion, and immersion in deviant social networks generated by earlier contact with the criminal justice system.

Chiricos et al. (2007) demonstrate that formal felony adjudication itself increases the likelihood of future conviction, even after accounting for prior behavior. This finding suggests that prior criminal record—used in the present study as an indicator of cumulative labeling—should be a particularly powerful predictor of rearrest during the pretrial period. As labeling becomes more entrenched through multiple arrests and convictions, the associated risks of pretrial failure are expected to rise accordingly.

Stolzenberg et al. (2021) further connect labeling processes to front-end decision-making by law enforcement. Using data from a random sample of criminal incidents in five jurisdictions between 2003 and 2006, they examined the relationship between suspects' prior criminal histories and the likelihood of arrest. After controlling for legally relevant factors, suspects with prior records were 29 times as likely to be arrested as those without prior records. The authors argue that this striking effect reflects not only officers' perceptions of culpability but also the stigmatizing influence of prior record on police behavior: once labeled, individuals become more visible to authorities and more vulnerable to formal sanction.

Pretrial detention itself may deepen these labeling effects. Individuals who remain in jail because they cannot afford bail are effectively treated as criminals before conviction. They frequently lose employment and housing, strain family relationships, and encounter intensified stigma upon release. For those ultimately convicted of a felony, the consequences are even more severe, including disenfranchisement, exclusion from jury service, firearm prohibitions, and disqualification from numerous public offices and occupations. These legal and social sanctions reinforce the criminal label and further restrict access to conventional opportunities.

The present study extends existing labeling research in several important respects. First, it moves beyond single-state or single-jurisdiction samples by employing data from 71 of the most populous urban counties in the United States, thereby capturing substantial variation in legal practices and social contexts. Second, it operationalizes "criminal record" more precisely by incorporating both arrests and convictions as indicators of cumulative labeling and prior system contact. Third, it directly evaluates whether criminal history is a more powerful predictor of pretrial failure than the statutory seriousness of the current charge—an issue of central importance for bail policy and risk assessment.

From a policy standpoint, labeling theory underscores the need for bail practices that reduce unwarranted stigma and prevent unnecessary pretrial detention. If prior criminal record is indeed a strong predictor of pretrial rearrest, courts have reason to consider it in assessing risk. At the same time, labeling theory cautions that repeated labeling and punitive responses can generate self-fulfilling cycles of exclusion and recidivism. Bail reforms that limit reliance on monetary conditions, reduce unnecessary detention, and avoid automatically equating prior record with unmanageable risk may help disrupt these cycles and promote a more equitable, evidence-based pretrial justice system.

Chapter 4:

Research Methods

The present study examines the extent to which a defendant's prior criminal history predicts pretrial failure, with particular attention to rearrest while on bail and failure to appear. Although criminal history has long been recognized as one of the most consistent predictors of future criminal behavior, its role in bail determinations remains surprisingly limited in many jurisdictions. The analysis, therefore, incorporates a comprehensive set of control variables—including offense characteristics, demographic attributes, and other legally relevant factors—that may influence the likelihood of pretrial failure. Accounting for these factors is essential; without appropriate controls, any observed association between criminal history and pretrial outcomes could reflect omitted-variable bias rather than the independent contribution of prior convictions (D'Alessio & Stolzenberg, 2021).

By carefully isolating the effect of prior criminal history, this study evaluates whether a criminal record constitutes a more robust predictor of pretrial failure than the statutory seriousness of the current charge, net of other relevant influences. Importantly, the analysis does not presume that a prior record is inherently causal. Rather, it tests whether its predictive performance exceeds that of offense severity, given the available data and the specified statistical models.

The implications of this inquiry are both practical and significant. If prior criminal history outperforms offense severity as a predictor of pretrial failure, such evidence directly challenges the continued reliance on charge-based bail schedules and the dominance of monetary bail in pretrial decision-making. Cash bail functions primarily as a wealth screen rather than as a calibrated measure of risk, enabling defendants with financial resources to secure release while detaining indigent defendants who may pose little threat to public safety. By contrast, greater emphasis on prior criminal history aligns more closely with legally recognized risk considerations, including the likelihood of flight and potential danger to the community.

Emphasizing prior record in bail determinations also represents a feasible reform strategy. Unlike actuarial risk assessment instruments that rely on complex algorithms and proprietary data inputs, criminal history is transparent, standardized, and readily accessible to justice system actors. Its use reduces opportunities for subjective distortion while promoting greater consistency across defendants and jurisdictions, even as courts retain discretion to consider individualized circumstances when appropriate. Given its accessibility, legal relevance, and demonstrated predictive utility, prior criminal history offers an empirically grounded and administratively efficient alternative to the prevailing charge-based, financially driven bail framework. The findings of this study, therefore, contribute directly to ongoing policy debates concerning bail reform and the future of pretrial justice.

Data Source

This study draws on data from the 2009 State Court Processing Statistics (SCPS) program, administered by the Bureau of Justice Statistics (BJS) (Bureau of Justice Statistics, 2014). The SCPS program provides nationally representative information on felony defendants prosecuted in the 40 most populous urban counties in the United States and employs a two-stage stratified sampling design in which felony cases filed during a single month are randomly selected within sampled counties and then followed for approximately one year (Reaves, 2013). This design allows for systematic analysis of pretrial processing and case outcomes across jurisdictions while capturing key stages of criminal case progression, including bail decisions, pretrial release, rearrest, and failure to appear.

The 2009 SCPS dataset contains detailed case-level information on defendants' demographic characteristics, arrest charges, criminal histories, bail and pretrial release conditions, detention status, failure to appear, rearrest, adjudication outcomes, and sentencing decisions (Bureau of Justice Statistics, 2014). Although SCPS regularly samples 40 large urban counties, the present analysis is restricted to 35 counties that consistently report the full set of variables required to operationalize the study's dependent and independent measures. The 35 counties included in the analytic sample are listed in Appendix A.

The initial sample consists of 5974 felony defendants released on bail prior to trial in these 35 large urban counties, representing approximately 39% of all felony defendants processed in the SCPS 2009 cohort. After applying listwise deletion to retain only cases with complete data on all variables included in the multivariate models, the final analytic sample consists of 5322 defendants. All tables and figures presented in this study are based on this final analytic sample.

Overall levels of missing data were limited. Three control variables—race, type of legal representation, and time from arrest to release—exhibited higher rates of missingness. To preserve cases and avoid unnecessary sample loss, missing-indicator variables were incorporated for each of these measures prior to listwise deletion. This strategy reduces bias associated with case attrition while maintaining the integrity and comparability of the final analytic sample, in accordance with established practice in applied regression modeling (Allison, 2001; Cohen et al., 2003).

All data are publicly archived through the Inter-University Consortium for Political and Social Research (ICPSR) as part of the *State Court Processing Statistics, 1990–2009: Felony Defendants in Large Urban Counties (ICPSR 2038)* series, ensuring transparency, replicability, and long-term accessibility for researchers (Bureau of Justice Statistics, 2014).

Dependent Variables

The dependent variables in this study capture two core dimensions of pretrial failure: pretrial rearrest and failure to appear (FTA). Each outcome is operationalized as a dichotomous measure. For pretrial rearrest, defendants who were released before trial and subsequently rearrested for a new offense during the follow-up period are coded 1, and those not rearrested are coded 0. For failure to appear, defendants who missed a scheduled court appearance while on pretrial release are coded 1, and those who appeared as required are coded 0 (Dobbie et al., 2018).

Pretrial rearrest represents a particularly serious form of pretrial failure because it directly implicates public safety and has long served as a central constitutional justification for pretrial detention (Koepke & Robinson, 2018). Failure to appear, by contrast, reflects the court's institutional interest in ensuring compliance with judicial proceedings and the efficient administration of justice. Modeling these outcomes separately allows the analysis to evaluate whether the same factors—most notably prior criminal history—operate similarly across distinct dimensions of pretrial risk.

Although some FTAs may arise from logistical barriers such as transportation difficulties, childcare responsibilities, or scheduling conflicts (Goldkamp, 1980), contemporary pretrial research recognizes the importance of examining both rearrest and court-appearance behavior when evaluating bail policy and pretrial decision-making. Treating these outcomes independently, therefore, yields a more comprehensive and policy-relevant assessment of pretrial performance.

Key Independent Variable

The key independent variable of interest is the defendant's prior criminal history, a construct consistently identified as one of the strongest predictors of future offending and pretrial misconduct (D'Alessio & Stolzenberg, 2021). The SCPS dataset provides several discrete indicators of prior criminal involvement, allowing for a nuanced and theoretically meaningful assessment of criminal history. These indicators include total prior arrests, prior felony arrests, prior misdemeanor arrests, total prior convictions, prior felony convictions, prior misdemeanor convictions, prior prison incarcerations, and prior jail incarcerations. Each captures a distinct dimension of justice system contact: arrest variables reflect exposure to policing; conviction variables represent legally adjudicated culpability; and incarceration variables capture the most severe forms of penal intervention. Prior research demonstrates that conviction-based measures possess greater predictive validity for recidivism than arrest counts or incarceration history because convictions reflect substantiated wrongdoing rather than unadjudicated suspicion (Kleck & Barnes, 2010).

To identify the most representative and empirically robust measure of criminal history, a principal components analysis (PCA) was conducted using all available SCPS criminal history indicators. PCA is a well-established dimensionality-reduction technique widely used in criminology to uncover latent constructs underlying highly correlated measures of prior offending (Nagin & Pogarsky, 2001). The analysis revealed that the component dominated by total prior convictions accounted for approximately 90% of the variance across the criminal history indicators, making it the most influential and conceptually coherent representation of prior offending (see Figure 1). This result is consistent with long-standing research demonstrating that the number of prior convictions—particularly when combining felony and misdemeanor convictions—captures both the frequency and persistence of criminal activity, two key predictors of future misconduct (Sampson & Laub, 1993).

Based on these findings, the analysis operationalizes criminal history as the total number of prior convictions. In the SCPS data, this measure is coded as a discrete count variable ranging from 0 to 10+, with the highest category representing defendants with ten or more prior convictions. Collapsing extreme values into a 10+ category is standard practice in criminal justice research because high-frequency offenders constitute a small proportion of the population but exert disproportionate influence on statistical distributions (Sweeten et al., 2013). This approach also conforms to SCPS documentation protocols, which top-code extreme values to preserve confidentiality.

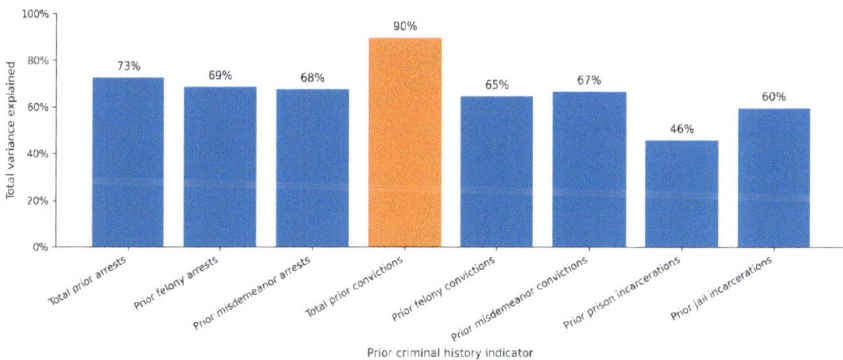

Figure 1. Predictive strength of alternative criminal history measures for pretrial failure in 35 U.S. counties (N = 5322).

Notes. Bars display the proportion of total variance in pretrial failure explained by each criminal history indicator. Total prior convictions are the single most powerful predictor, accounting for approximately 90% of the variance in the full set of criminal history measures. Arrest-based indicators and prior incarceration measures explain substantially less variation, underscoring that conviction-based criminal history—rather than arrests or prior detention—is the dominant empirical signal of pretrial risk.

Control Variables

To estimate the independent association between prior convictions and pretrial failure, the models include a comprehensive set of legally and empirically relevant control variables capturing offense seriousness, bail amount, number of arrest charges, criminal justice status at arrest, type of legal representation, time from arrest to release, and demographic characteristics. Including these controls is essential because each factor is known to influence pretrial outcomes, and omitting them could bias estimates of the relationship between criminal history and pretrial misconduct.

Together, these controls allow the analysis to isolate the predictive contribution of prior criminal history while accounting for alternative legal and social influences on pretrial behavior.

Offense Seriousness

Because offense severity is a core determinant of both judicial decision-making and pretrial behavior, the analysis explicitly controls for offense seriousness. Rather than imposing a single ordinal severity scale, offense seriousness is operationalized using five mutually exclusive offense categories: violent offenses, serious property offenses, minor property offenses, drug offenses, and public-order offenses. This categorical approach avoids arbitrary assumptions about the relative spacing of offense types and allows the model to capture meaningful differences across major classes of crime.

In the regression analyses, public-order offenses serve as the reference category; therefore, coefficients for the remaining categories represent differences in the odds of pretrial rearrest or failure to appear relative to defendants charged with public-order offenses. This specification provides a transparent and flexible control for offense seriousness while preserving interpretability and consistency across models.

Bail Amount

The bail amount is included as a continuous control variable and is natural-log transformed to address the substantial right skew in the distribution of monetary bail. Log transformation is standard practice when modeling highly skewed financial variables, as it allows the estimated effects to be interpreted as proportional rather than absolute changes.

Prior research demonstrates that higher bail amounts are associated with increased risks of pretrial failure, reflecting both judicial assessments of defendant risk and the destabilizing effects of financial strain on defendants and their families (D'Alessio & Stolzenberg, 2021). Bail also operates as a structural barrier to release for low-income defendants. Those unable to post bond often experience more extended periods of detention, greater disruption of employment and family stability, and closer supervision following release—conditions that may increase the likelihood of rearrest and other forms of pretrial failure (Heaton et al., 2017).

By modeling the bail amount in a log form, the analysis reduces the influence of extreme values, improves model fit, and more accurately captures the nonlinear relationship between the financial conditions of release and pretrial outcomes.

Arrest Charges

The number of arrest charges is measured as a count variable capturing the breadth of alleged criminal conduct in the current case. Defendants facing multiple charges often experience heightened judicial scrutiny and more intensive supervision, which increases the likelihood that violations of release conditions will be detected and formally recorded (Tartaro & Sedelmaier, 2009).

Beyond its legal significance, a larger number of charges may also contribute to greater legal uncertainty, psychological stress, and disruption of social and economic stability—factors associated with elevated risks of pretrial misconduct. Including this measure allows the analysis to distinguish the effect of the volume of current charges from the effect of a defendant's accumulated criminal history, thereby improving the precision of the estimated relationship between prior convictions and pretrial failure.

Criminal Justice Status at Arrest

A defendant's criminal justice status at the time of arrest is included as a single dichotomous indicator, coded 1 if the defendant was under any form of active criminal justice supervision at the time of arrest (e.g., probation, parole, release on a pending case, in custody, diversion, or fugitive status), and 0 otherwise. Defendants under supervision consistently exhibit higher rates of pretrial misconduct, in part because supervision status reflects recent criminal involvement, ongoing legal obligations, and heightened structural surveillance that increases the probability of detecting new offenses (Cohen & Reaves, 2007).

Individuals under supervision are also subject to additional restrictions and technical conditions, making them more vulnerable to formal violations for conduct that might not result in arrest among unsupervised defendants. Controlling for criminal justice status at arrest is therefore essential to avoid overstating the independent effect of prior criminal history on pretrial failure.

Legal Representation

Legal representation is measured as a dichotomous variable indicating whether the defendant was represented by a court-appointed attorney (coded 1) or by a private attorney (coded 0). This measure is included because the type of counsel is strongly associated with underlying socioeconomic status, which, in turn, is closely linked to patterns of criminal justice involvement and the risk of pretrial failure (Hanson, 2003).

Defendants assigned court-appointed counsel are, on average, more economically disadvantaged and more likely to experience unstable employment, housing insecurity, and limited access to supportive resources—conditions that may elevate the risk of pretrial rearrest and failure to appear (Harlow, 2000). Including this measure, therefore, allows the analysis to control, albeit imperfectly, for important social and economic differences among defendants that are not directly observed in the SCPS data.

Because information on legal representation exhibits higher levels of missingness than most other covariates, a corresponding missing-indicator variable is included in the models for this measure. This strategy preserves cases and reduces the likelihood that estimates are biased by systematic case attrition associated with unobserved socioeconomic disadvantage.

Time to Release

Time to release, measured as the number of days between arrest and pretrial release, captures the temporal dimension of pretrial detention. Because the distribution of detention length is highly right-skewed, this variable is entered into the models in natural-log form to reduce the influence of extreme values and to better approximate a linear relationship with pretrial outcomes.

Extensive research demonstrates that even short periods of pretrial detention can destabilize employment, disrupt family relationships, and exacerbate mental health challenges—processes that independently increase the risk of subsequent criminal behavior (Dobbie et al., 2018). Longer detention periods may also generate labeling effects and weaken prosocial bonds, further elevating the likelihood of rearrest or court noncompliance following release. Including time to release, therefore, helps isolate the effect of prior criminal history from the criminogenic consequences of pretrial confinement itself.

Because the time-to-release variable exhibits higher levels of missingness, a corresponding indicator variable for missingness is incorporated into the models for this measure. This approach preserves cases and reduces the risk that estimated effects are driven by systematic sample attrition.

Demographic Characteristics

Demographic characteristics are included as control variables because of their well-established relationships with criminal involvement, system contact, and pretrial outcomes. Age is a robust predictor of criminal behavior, with offending rates peaking in late adolescence and early adulthood and declining steadily thereafter (Piquero et al., 2015). Accordingly, age is included as a continuous measure in years at the time of arrest.

Race and Hispanic ethnicity are incorporated because longstanding patterns of differential policing, surveillance, and structural disadvantage contribute to racial and ethnic disparities in rearrest and pretrial processing that may operate independently of criminal history (McGovern et al., 2009). Race is measured using dichotomous indicators with White defendants as the reference category, and a separate missing-data indicator is included for defendants whose race information is not reported in the SCPS data. Hispanic ethnicity is measured dichotomously (1 = Hispanic, 0 = non-Hispanic).

Gender is also controlled because males consistently exhibit higher rates of criminal offending and pretrial misconduct than females (Steffensmeier et al., 2005). Gender is coded dichotomously (1 = male, 0 = female).

Including these demographic characteristics ensures that observed associations between prior criminal history and pretrial failure are not confounded by population-level differences in age structure, gender composition, or racially patterned exposure to criminal justice intervention.

County Fixed Effects

All regression models include county fixed effects to control for unobserved heterogeneity across jurisdictions. Counties differ substantially in bail practices, court resources, policing intensity, prosecutorial norms, pretrial services, and local legal culture. Failing to account for these structural differences could confound estimates of individual-level predictors.

By including a full set of county indicator variables (not shown in the tables), the models control for all stable county-specific characteristics, ensuring that the estimated effects of criminal history and other covariates reflect within-county variation rather than cross-county differences in policy or practice. This specification strengthens causal inference and improves the internal validity of the estimated relationships.

Analytical Strategy

This study employs binary logistic regression estimated in SPSS Version 25 (IBM Corp., 2017) to evaluate whether a defendant's prior criminal history predicts pretrial failure, defined as (1) pretrial rearrest and (2) failure to appear (FTA) among defendants released before trial. Logistic regression is appropriate because both dependent variables are dichotomous and because the method imposes no assumption of normally distributed errors while accommodating predictors measured at nominal, ordinal, and continuous levels (Hosmer et al., 2013). This modeling framework is standard in criminological research for estimating recidivism, pretrial misconduct, and other binary outcomes.

Model coefficients represent the effect of each predictor on the log odds of pretrial failure. Because log-odds are not readily interpretable, coefficients are exponentiated to obtain odds ratios (e^b). Odds ratios greater than 1.0 indicate an increased likelihood of pretrial failure, whereas values below 1.0 indicate a decreased likelihood. To convey substantive magnitude, results are expressed as percentage changes in the odds, calculated as $100(e^b - 1)$, where e^b denotes the exponentiated coefficient (Long & Freese, 2014). This transformation allows direct interpretation of how a one-unit change in a predictor alters the probability of pretrial failure.

All hypothesis tests use a conventional two-tailed alpha of .05, consistent with established standards in criminal justice research

(Agresti, 2018). Model diagnostics were examined to assess coefficient stability and whether any single variable exerted undue influence on parameter estimates.

The analysis proceeds in two stages. First, descriptive statistics and bivariate associations are examined for the two focal predictors— offense seriousness and total prior convictions—to document their distributions and unadjusted relationships with each pretrial outcome. Second, a series of multivariate logistic regression models are estimated to assess the independent effect of prior criminal history on pretrial rearrest and FTA while simultaneously controlling for all legal, demographic, and contextual covariates specified in the research design.

This structured modeling strategy enables both preliminary pattern identification and rigorous multivariate hypothesis testing, consistent with best practices in quantitative criminology (Bachman & Schutt, 2020). Together, these procedures provide a robust evaluation of whether a prior criminal record predicts pretrial failure, net of offense severity and other legally relevant factors, thereby directly addressing the study's central research question.

Model Diagnostics and Assumption Checks

To ensure the robustness and validity of the logistic regression estimates, a comprehensive set of diagnostic procedures and assumption checks was conducted in accordance with best practices in applied statistical modeling (Hosmer et al., 2013). Although logistic regression does not require the assumptions of normality, homoscedasticity, or linearity in the dependent variable associated with ordinary least squares regression, careful evaluation of model fit, multicollinearity, influential observations, and the functional form of predictors remains essential.

Multicollinearity was assessed using variance inflation factors (VIFs) and tolerance statistics for all predictors. VIF values below the commonly accepted threshold of 10 and tolerance values well above 0.10 indicate that collinearity does not pose a threat to the stability of the coefficient estimates (O'Brien, 2007). These results were consistent with expectations, particularly given that the earlier principal components analysis identified and reduced redundancy among criminal history indicators.

Overall model fit was evaluated using multiple complementary indices. The Hosmer–Lemeshow goodness-of-fit test was employed to assess whether observed pretrial failure rates differed significantly from those predicted by the model across risk deciles. A non-significant Hosmer–Lemeshow statistic indicates adequate model fit, suggesting that predicted probabilities correspond closely with observed outcomes (Hosmer et al., 2013).

In addition, pseudo-R^2 statistics, including the Cox & Snell and Nagelkerke measures, were examined to assess the relative explanatory power of competing model specifications. Although pseudo-R^2 values do not share the same interpretation as R^2 in linear regression, they provide useful comparative information regarding improvements in model performance as additional predictors are introduced (Menard, 2010).

The model's ability to discriminate between defendants who experienced pretrial failure and those who did not was evaluated using the area under the receiver operating characteristic (ROC) curve (AUC). AUC values closer to 1.0 indicate stronger classification performance, with values above 0.70 generally considered acceptable in applied criminal justice research (Rice & Harris, 2005). This statistic provides an important measure of the model's practical utility for identifying defendants at elevated risk of pretrial failure.

The assumption of linearity between continuous predictors and the log-odds of pretrial failure was tested using the Box–Tidwell procedure, which assesses whether the interaction between each continuous predictor and its natural logarithm is statistically significant (Box & Tidwell, 1962). Non-significant interaction terms support the linearity assumption. Where violations might have been detected, transformations or categorical specifications would have been considered (Long & Freese, 2014).

Finally, the presence of influential cases was examined using standardized residuals, Cook's distance, and leverage values. Observations with standardized residuals exceeding ±2.5 standard deviations, Cook's D values above 1.0, or unusually high leverage can exert disproportionate influence on coefficient estimates and warrant further scrutiny (Belsley et al., 1980). No evidence of undue influence was detected.

Collectively, these diagnostic checks indicate that the logistic regression models are well specified, stable, and statistically sound. The absence of problematic multicollinearity, satisfactory model fit, acceptable classification accuracy, and compliance with key assumptions support the reliability of the estimated effects and the substantive conclusions drawn regarding pretrial failure.

Summary of Analytic Approach

In summary, the analytic strategy employed in this study was designed to rigorously evaluate whether a defendant's prior criminal record independently predicts the likelihood of pretrial failure, operationalized as rearrest during the pretrial period. The analysis began with careful attention to data quality, variable construction, and the dimensionality of the criminal history indicators. A principal components analysis was conducted to identify the most conceptually coherent and statistically dominant representation of criminal history, yielding total prior convictions as the primary independent variable.

Descriptive statistics and bivariate associations were then examined to establish baseline patterns and to explore preliminary relationships among offense seriousness, prior convictions, and pretrial rearrest. These exploratory analyses provided essential context for understanding the data structure and informed the specification of the multivariate model.

The core empirical test employed binary logistic regression, a method well-suited for modeling dichotomous outcomes and estimating the effects of both continuous and categorical predictors. This approach enabled the analysis to control simultaneously for a comprehensive set of legal, demographic, socioeconomic, and supervisory variables known to influence pretrial outcomes. Coefficients were interpreted using odds ratios to facilitate substantive interpretation of effect sizes, with a conventional two-tailed significance threshold of .05 guiding statistical inference.

To verify the validity and reliability of the findings, extensive diagnostic procedures were conducted. These included assessments of multicollinearity, model fit, classification accuracy, logit linearity, and influential observations. Collectively, the diagnostics indicated that the final model was specified correctly, statistically stable, and consistent with the core assumptions of logistic regression.

Through this multi-stage analytical process—encompassing rigorous measurement, careful model specification, and systematic diagnostic evaluation—the study provides a strong empirical foundation for assessing whether criminal history is a more reliable predictor of pretrial risk than offense severity. The following chapter presents the results of these analyses and discusses their implications for pretrial decision-making and bail reform policy.

Chapter 5:

Study Findings

This chapter presents the empirical findings from both descriptive and multivariate analyses examining the factors associated with pretrial failure, defined as pretrial rearrest and failure to appear (FTA). The analysis examines whether a defendant's prior criminal history remains a dominant predictor of pretrial outcomes after controlling for offense characteristics, bail conditions, legal representation, supervision status, and demographic factors.

The chapter begins with descriptive results that document baseline patterns in pretrial outcomes and illustrate the bivariate relationships between criminal history, offense type, bail amount, and pretrial misconduct. These patterns provide essential context for the multivariate models that follow and highlight the central role of criminal history in shaping pretrial risk.

Table 2 then reports the logistic regression results for both dimensions of pretrial failure—pretrial rearrest and failure to appear (FTA)—estimated on a common analytic sample of 5322 defendants drawn from 35 large urban counties. Each model includes the complete set of legally relevant, demographic, and contextual control variables described in the preceding chapter, with county fixed effects incorporated to account for unobserved differences in local court practices and institutional conditions.

Together, these analyses provide a rigorous assessment of the relative importance of criminal history, offense severity, and bail conditions in predicting pretrial misconduct and offer direct empirical guidance for bail policy and pretrial decision-making.

Descriptive Analysis Results

Table 1 presents descriptive statistics for all variables used in the analysis. The final analytic sample consists of 5322 felony defendants from 35 large urban counties. Approximately 14% of defendants were rearrested during the pretrial period, and 14% failed to appear in court. These rates are consistent with national estimates of pretrial misconduct reported in prior State Court Processing Statistics studies, which typically range between 14% and 18%.

Table 1. Description of variables used in the analysis.

Variable	Proportion Mean (SD)	Sample Size	Definition
Pretrial rearrest	.14	5764	1=yes, 0=no
Pretrial FTA	.14	5765	1=yes, 0=no
Prior convictions	2.28 (3.17)	5961	Range 0-10+
Bail amount	22,076.68 (58,472.83)	5974	Range $10-2.5 million
Arrest charges	2.32 (2.64)	5752	Range 1-72 arrest charges
Male	.81	5901	1=male, 0=female
Age at arrest	31.27 (10.90)	5950	Range 15-83 years
Black	.51	5974	1=Black, 0=White
Black MI	.12	5974	1=missing, 0−no
Hispanic	.18	5974	1=Hispanic, 0=non-Hispanic
Court-appointed attorney	.57	5974	1=public defender/assigned attorney, 0=private attorney
Court-appointed attorney MI	.27	5974	1=missing, 0=no
CJ status at arrest	.20	5933	1=active (e.g., released prior case, probation, parole, in custody, diversion, fugitive), 0=none
Time to release	13.60 (33.45)	5974	Range 0-667 days

Variable	Proportion Mean (SD)	Sample Size	Definition
Time to release MI	.10	5974	1=missing, 0=no
Violent	.23	5950	1=yes, 0=no
Serious property	.10	5950	1=yes, 0=no
Minor property	.18	5950	1=yes, 0=no
Drug	.33	5950	1=yes, 0=no
Public order	.16	5950	1=yes, 0=no

Notes. N = 5322 defendants from 35 U.S. counties. SD = standard deviation. Variable-specific sample sizes reflect the number of non-missing observations prior to listwise deletion. All multivariate regression models are estimated using a common analytic sample (N = 5322), with listwise deletion applied to all model variables.

The central independent variable, total prior convictions, exhibits substantial variation (M = 2.28, SD = 3.17), with values ranging from 0 to 10 or more prior convictions. This heterogeneity is substantively important, given the extensive criminological literature identifying prior convictions as among the most powerful predictors of subsequent offending and supervision failure.

Bail amounts are highly dispersed, with a mean of $22,076.68 (SD = $58,472.83) and a range from $10 to $2.5 million, reflecting wide variation in offense severity and judicial practices across jurisdictions. The number of arrest charges also varies considerably (M = 2.32, SD = 2.64), ranging from 1 to 72 charges, underscoring substantial differences in case complexity and legal exposure at the time of arrest.

The sample is predominantly male (81%), with an average age at arrest of 31.27 years (SD = 10.90; range 15–83). Racial composition indicates that 51% of defendants are Black and 18% Hispanic, patterns consistent with long-documented racial disparities in felony case processing and incarceration. A majority of defendants (57%) were represented by court-appointed counsel, reflecting the strong relationship between socioeconomic disadvantage and criminal justice involvement. At arrest, 20% of defendants were under active criminal justice supervision. The average time from arrest to release was 13.60 days (SD = 33.45), with a maximum of 667 days, indicating wide variation in pretrial detention experiences.

Regarding offense composition, drug offenses constitute the largest category (33%), followed by violent offenses (23%), minor property offenses (18%), public order offenses (16%), and serious property offenses (10%). These distributions closely mirror national patterns in felony case processing.

Figure 2 demonstrates that both pretrial rearrest and failure-to-appear (FTA) rates remain largely insensitive to bail amount. Rearrest rates fluctuate narrowly between 12% and 16% across bail quintiles, while FTA rates range from 12% to 16%, showing no monotonic decline as bail increases. Notably, the highest bail quintile (top 20%) does not produce lower failure rates than the lowest quintile: rearrest remains approximately 16% and FTA approximately 12%, compared with 12% rearrest and 16% FTA in the lowest quintile. This pattern indicates that higher monetary bail does not meaningfully reduce either form of pretrial failure.

Figure 3 reveals a strong, graded relationship between prior convictions and both dimensions of pretrial failure. Rearrest increases from 10% among defendants with no prior convictions to 26% among those with 7 or 10+ prior convictions, while FTA rises from 12% to approximately 21–26% across the same range. The pattern is monotonic for both outcomes: as prior convictions accumulate, both rearrest and court nonappearance increase sharply, demonstrating a classic dose–response relationship. Criminal history, therefore, captures a general propensity toward pretrial noncompliance, affecting both criminal activity and appearance behavior.

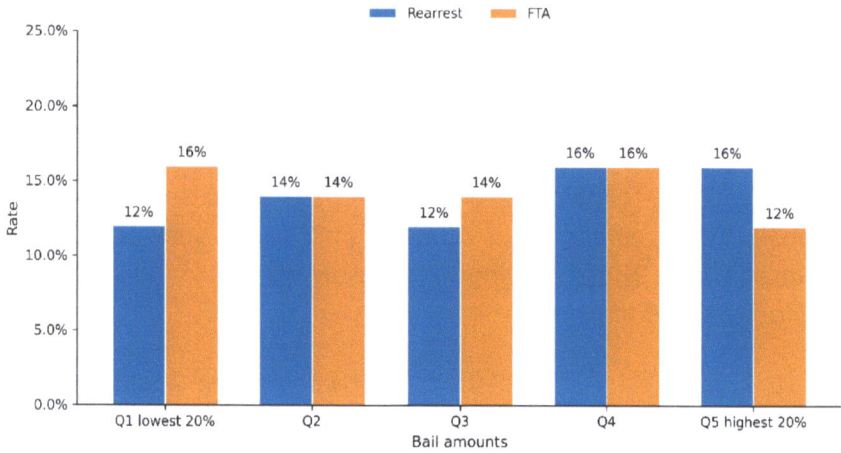

Figure 2. Pretrial rearrest and failure-to-appear (FTA) rates by bail amount in 35 U.S. counties (N = 5322).

Notes. Bars show the proportions of defendants who experience pretrial rearrest and FTA across bail quintiles. Both outcomes exhibit minimal variation across bail levels, indicating that higher monetary bail is not associated with lower pretrial failure.

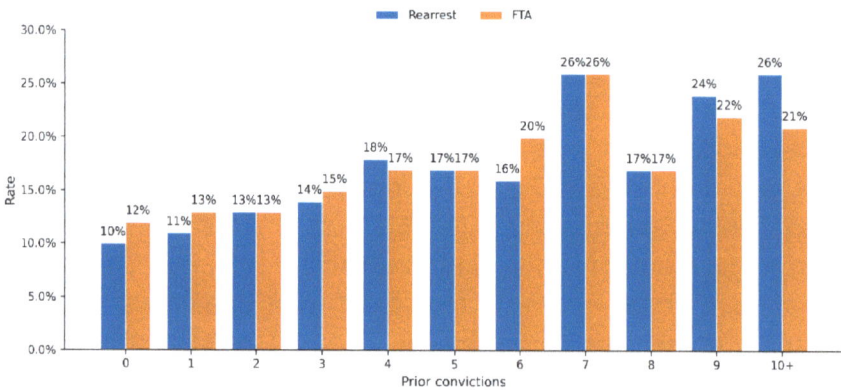

Figure 3. Pretrial rearrest and failure-to-appear (FTA) rates by number of prior convictions in 35 U.S. counties (N = 5322).

Notes. Rates of both rearrest and FTA increase monotonically with the accumulation of prior convictions, demonstrating a strong dose–response relationship between criminal history and pretrial failure.

Figure 4 shows that prior convictions strongly stratify risk across all offense categories for both outcomes. Among defendants without prior convictions, rearrest rates range from 9–11% and FTA rates range from 8–13%. Among defendants with prior convictions, rearrest increases to 13–17% and FTA to 11–18%, depending on offense type. The largest differentials appear among nonviolent defendants, with rearrest rising from 11% to 17% and FTA from 13% to 18% when criminal history is present. These patterns indicate that criminal history differentiates pretrial risk far more sharply than offense severity alone.

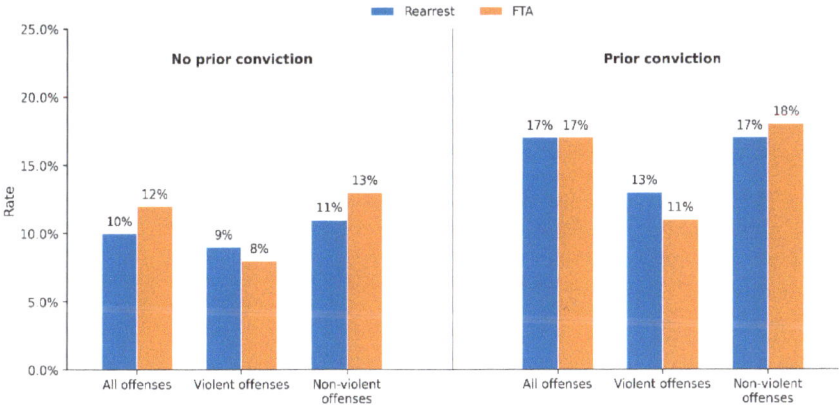

Figure 4. Pretrial rearrest and failure-to-appear (FTA) rates by offense type and prior conviction status in 35 U.S. counties (N = 5322).

Notes. Within each offense category, defendants with prior convictions exhibit substantially higher rates of both rearrest and FTA than defendants without prior convictions, highlighting the dominant role of criminal history in stratifying pretrial risk.

Figure 5 illustrates variation in both outcomes across offense types, but again reveals the limited predictive value of charge severity. Rearrest is highest for serious property offenses (21%), followed by minor property (15%), drug (13%), and public order (12%), while violent offenses show the lowest rearrest rate (10%). FTA follows a similar pattern: serious property (19%), drug (16%), minor property (16%), public order (14%), and violent offenses (10%). The fact that defendants charged with violent offenses display the lowest failure rates on both dimensions further underscores the weakness of offense severity as a proxy for short-term pretrial risk.

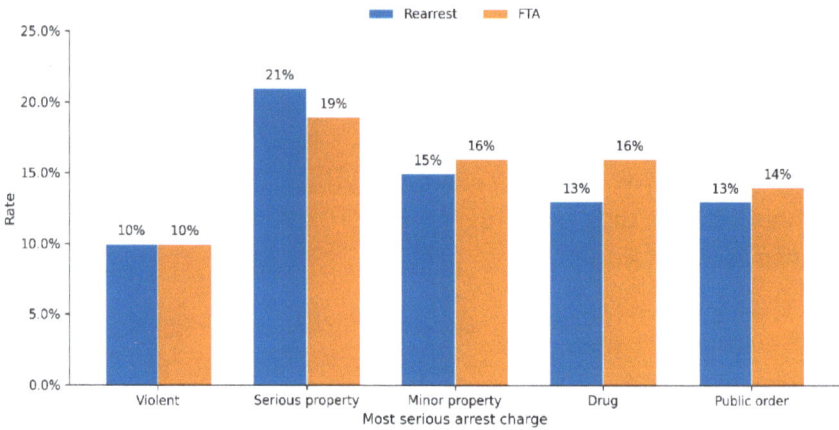

Figure 5. Pretrial rearrest and failure-to-appear (FTA) rates by most serious arrest charge in 35 U.S. counties (N = 5322).

Notes. Pretrial failure varies across offense types, but defendants charged with violent offenses display the lowest rates of both rearrest and FTA, underscoring the limited predictive value of charge severity for short-term pretrial outcomes.

Taken together, these descriptive patterns reveal a clear empirical structure: pretrial failure is driven far more by accumulated criminal history than by either the monetary conditions of release or the statutory seriousness of the current charge. Bail levels exhibit no meaningful association with either rearrest or failure to appear (FTA), while offense severity produces inconsistent and often counterintuitive patterns. In contrast, prior convictions generate large, monotonic increases in both dimensions of pretrial failure.

These findings motivate the multivariate analyses that follow. However, the descriptive results do not account for the simultaneous influence of offense characteristics, bail conditions, legal representation, demographic factors, and other legally relevant covariates. Because bivariate associations alone cannot establish whether the observed relationship between criminal history and pretrial outcomes reflects an independent effect or is driven by confounding relationships with these competing factors, a more rigorous analytical framework is required.

Accordingly, the following section presents multivariate logistic regression models estimating the independent effects of criminal history, offense type, bail amount, and the full set of control variables on the likelihood of both pretrial rearrest and failure to appear. By isolating the contribution of each predictor while holding all others constant, the models provide a stringent test of whether prior convictions remain the most consequential determinant of pretrial misconduct.

Logistic Regression Results

Table 2 reports multivariate logistic regression results predicting both dimensions of pretrial failure—pretrial rearrest and failure to appear (FTA)—for a common analytic sample of 5322 defendants from 35 large urban counties. Each model includes the full set of legally relevant, demographic, and contextual controls, with county fixed effects included to account for unobserved institutional differences across jurisdictions. To preserve the analytic sample and minimize bias from item nonresponse, missing-indicator variables were incorporated for race, court-appointed counsel, and time to release; the effects of these indicators are interpreted alongside the substantive covariates.

Table 2. Logistic regression results predicting pretrial failure to appear and rearrest.

Variable	Rearrest Odds Ratio	SE	FTA Odds Ratio	SE
Prior convictions	1.111***	.014	1.059***	.014
Bail amount (ln)	1.066	.039	.872***	.038
Arrest charges	1.036**	.014	.998	.018
Male	1.275*	.119	1.141	.114
Age at arrest	.974***	.005	.991*	.004
Black	1.112	.103	1.148	.102

| | Rearrest | | FTA | |
Variable	Odds Ratio	SE	Odds Ratio	SE
Black MI	1.318	.193	.762	.184
Hispanic	.831	.143	1.258	.134
Court-appointed attorney	1.182	.112	1.680***	.115
Court-appointed attorney MI	.938	.103	2.088***	.097
CJ status at arrest	1.531***	.101	1.355**	.101
Time to release (ln)	1.119**	.036	1.091*	.036
Time to release MI	1.032	.216	1.156	.185
Violent	.680**	.152	.687**	.152
Serious property	1.450*	.161	1.213	.162
Minor property	1.236	.149	1.132	.145
Drug	.846	.134	1.062	.128
Constant	.062***	.479	.153***	.446
Nagelkerke R^2	.131		.143	

Notes. $*p \leq 0.05$; $**p \leq 0.01$; $***p \leq 0.001$ (two-tailed tests). N = 5322 defendants from 35 U.S. counties. SE = standard error. County fixed effects are included in the regression models but not shown in the table. The final analytic sample uses listwise deletion across all variables included in the regression models.

Across both models, prior criminal history emerges as the strongest and most consistent predictor of pretrial failure. Each additional prior conviction increases the odds of pretrial rearrest by approximately 11% and the odds of FTA by approximately 6%, net of all other factors. No other predictor in either model approaches this level of magnitude or consistency. Because prior convictions are measured as a count variable, the effect is cumulative: defendants with extensive criminal records face sharply elevated risks of both new offending and court nonappearance. These results confirm that an accumulated criminal record captures persistent behavioral risk far more effectively than either charge severity or monetary conditions.

Logged bail amount does not significantly predict pretrial rearrest; the odds ratio remains close to 1.0, indicating that higher bail does not meaningfully reduce the risk of new criminal activity while on release. In contrast, bail amount significantly reduces the likelihood of FTA: higher bail is associated with lower odds of missing court, confirming that money bail primarily operates as a court-attendance compliance mechanism rather than a public-safety intervention.

Defendants under active criminal justice supervision at the time of arrest face a sharply elevated risk of both outcomes. Supervised defendants experienced over 50% higher odds of rearrest and over 35% higher odds of FTA compared to unsupervised defendants. This reflects both underlying behavioral risk and the intensified surveillance that accompanies formal supervision.

The logged time from arrest to release significantly predicts both rearrest and FTA. Longer detention prior to release increases the odds of both forms of pretrial failure, reinforcing evidence that pretrial detention itself is criminogenic. The corresponding missing-indicator for time to release is not statistically significant for either outcome, indicating that cases with missing detention information do not differ systematically from observed cases after controlling for other covariates. This supports the validity of the missing-indicator strategy and suggests that the estimated detention effects are not driven by sample attrition.

Defendants represented by court-appointed counsel are nearly 70% more likely to fail to appear than defendants with private attorneys, net of all other factors. This strong relationship highlights the role of socioeconomic disadvantage and resource constraints in shaping procedural compliance. The missing-indicator for legal representation is also highly significant for FTA, with defendants whose representation information is missing exhibiting more than double the odds of failing to appear. This pattern strongly suggests that missingness in counsel data is itself informative and associated with elevated procedural risk. Neither representation nor its missing-indicator significantly predicts rearrest, indicating that counsel primarily influences court compliance rather than criminal behavior.

Once criminal history and structural controls are included, offense categories exhibit weak and inconsistent effects across both outcomes. Violent charges are associated with a lower risk of both rearrest and FTA, while serious property offenses increase rearrest risk. Most offense categories do not reach statistical significance. These results confirm that charge severity is a poor proxy for actual pretrial risk, especially relative to accumulated criminal history.

Age is consistently protective: older defendants are significantly less likely to be rearrested or to miss court. Male defendants face a significantly higher risk of rearrest. Race and ethnicity do not reach statistical significance once legal and structural controls are included. The missing-indicator for race is not significant for either outcome, indicating that unobserved race information does not introduce systematic bias into the estimated relationships.

Both models exhibit typical explanatory power for individual-level criminal behavior, with Nagelkerke R^2 values of approximately 0.13–0.14 and strong internal consistency across outcomes. Taken together, the results demonstrate that prior criminal history is the only predictor that is simultaneously strong, consistent, and substantively meaningful. Monetary bail, offense severity, and many traditional release criteria perform far more weakly and inconsistently. The inclusion and interpretation of missing-data indicators confirm that the core findings are not artifacts of sample attrition but reflect stable behavioral and structural relationships. Overall, the models show that pretrial risk is driven primarily by accumulated criminal record and structural constraints, rather than by the seriousness of the current charge or the amount of money required for release.

The findings presented in this chapter carry clear and far-reaching implications for the structure of pretrial decision-making in the United States. The empirical evidence demonstrates that prior criminal history is by far the most powerful and reliable predictor of pretrial failure across both rearrest and failure-to-appear outcomes, even after controlling for offense type, bail amount, detention time, supervision status, legal representation, and demographic characteristics, as well as fixed differences across counties. By contrast, the seriousness of the current charge and the amount of money imposed for release exhibit weak, inconsistent, and often misleading relationships with actual pretrial risk.

These results challenge the foundational logic of prevailing bail practices. Charge-based bail schedules and monetary release conditions dominate pretrial processing in most jurisdictions, yet the present analysis shows that they perform poorly as tools for identifying individuals who pose the greatest risk of pretrial misconduct. Instead, pretrial risk is structured primarily by defendants' accumulated criminal records and by the destabilizing effects of detention and structural disadvantage. In effect, contemporary bail systems rely heavily on criteria that are only weakly related to the outcomes they are intended to prevent.

This misalignment between policy and evidence has serious consequences. By anchoring pretrial decisions to offense severity and financial capacity rather than to empirically grounded risk indicators, current bail practices systematically detain many low-risk individuals while allowing some higher-risk defendants to secure release solely on their ability to pay. The result is a pretrial regime that undermines both public safety and procedural fairness, while imposing substantial social and economic costs on defendants, families, and communities.

The next chapter examines how these findings should reshape pretrial policy. It considers the implications for bail schedules, monetary release, risk assessment, detention practices, and the broader goals of fairness, safety, and constitutional legitimacy in pretrial justice.

Chapter 6:

Discussion and Implications

This chapter interprets the study's multivariate findings and situates them within the broader literature on pretrial risk, bail reform, and contemporary criminal justice policy. It examines how the results refine existing theoretical and empirical understandings of pretrial failure, identifies the study's key limitations, and outlines directions for future research. The chapter concludes with a set of policy implications grounded directly in the evidence presented in the preceding chapters.

Discussion

The findings of this study provide strong and consistent evidence that prior criminal history is the most powerful predictor of pretrial rearrest among felony defendants in large urban jurisdictions. Both the descriptive patterns and the multivariate models demonstrate that the number of prior convictions has a stronger and more consistent effect on pretrial misconduct than any other variable examined. This result reinforces a substantial body of criminological research identifying criminal history as a highly reliable indicator of future offending because it captures the persistence, frequency, and seriousness of past behavior (Piquero et al., 2015).

By contrast, offense severity—long treated as a central organizing principle of bail schedules and judicial decision-making—exhibits limited predictive value once other factors are held constant. Although defendants charged with property and drug offenses displayed higher rearrest rates than those charged with homicide in the descriptive analyses, these differences did not reach statistical significance in the multivariate models. The large standard errors associated with homicide charges reflect the small size of that reference group, but the substantive implication is clear: the seriousness of the charged offense does not reliably predict short-term pretrial risk. This pattern is consistent with prior research showing that individuals charged with serious violent offenses often recidivate at lower rates during the pretrial period than chronic property and drug offenders, directly challenging the assumptions that underlie offense-based bail schedules (Bechtel et al., 2011).

The results also reveal a striking disconnect between monetary bail and public safety. Bail amount—entered in logged form to correct for skew—exerts no meaningful effect on pretrial rearrest. The odds ratio remains near unity, indicating that increasing bail does not reduce the likelihood of new criminal activity while on release. This finding aligns with a growing empirical consensus that monetary bail fails to prevent crime and instead operates primarily as a wealth-based detention mechanism that deepens inequality without enhancing public safety (Monaghan et al., 2022). The absence of a protective effect of bail in this study provides robust empirical support for jurisdictions seeking alternatives to money bail.

Several legally relevant structural factors, however, remain strongly associated with pretrial rearrest. Defendants under active criminal justice supervision at the time of arrest were substantially more likely to be rearrested, a pattern consistent with theories of cumulative disadvantage and surveillance exposure, which emphasize that supervised individuals face heightened monitoring and greater vulnerability to detection for new offenses and technical violations (Cohen & Reaves, 2007). Similarly, longer pretrial detention—measured as logged time from arrest to release—significantly increased the likelihood of rearrest, reinforcing recent scholarship documenting the destabilizing and criminogenic effects of even short periods of jail confinement (Dobbie et al., 2018). Together, these findings underscore the extent to which institutional processes themselves shape pretrial outcomes.

Legal representation also plays an important role in pretrial behavior. Defendants represented by court-appointed counsel were significantly more likely to be rearrested than those with private attorneys. This pattern likely reflects underlying socioeconomic disadvantage, including unstable employment, housing insecurity, and limited access to supportive resources, rather than differences in attorney performance per se (Hanson, 2003). The result highlights how structural inequality continues to influence pretrial outcomes even after controlling for offense characteristics, criminal history, and other legal factors.

Demographic variables behave in predictable ways. Younger defendants and males face higher risks of pretrial rearrest, consistent with well-established age–crime and gender patterns in offending (Piquero et al., 2015). Race and Hispanic ethnicity do not achieve statistical significance in the multivariate model, though their directional effects remain consistent with broader research documenting racialized patterns of system contact rooted in structural inequality and differential surveillance (Gase et al., 2016).

Taken together, the findings present a coherent and theoretically grounded account of pretrial risk. Accumulated criminal history stands apart as the most reliable predictor of pretrial misconduct, while offense severity and monetary bail contribute little meaningful explanatory power. These results directly challenge the logic of charge-based bail schedules and wealth-based detention practices and underscore the necessity of shifting pretrial decision-making toward empirically grounded, risk-informed, and equity-centered frameworks.

Policy Implications for Bail Reform

The results of this study carry direct and substantial implications for the design of pretrial policy and the future of bail reform in the United States. Together, the findings demonstrate that many of the assumptions underlying current bail practices—particularly the emphasis on charge severity and monetary conditions—are poorly aligned with empirical realities of pretrial risk. Several clear policy directions follow.

First, jurisdictions should substantially reduce, and where possible eliminate, the use of monetary bail. The analysis shows that bail amount does not meaningfully predict pretrial rearrest, indicating that financial conditions of release do not enhance public safety. Instead, monetary bail functions primarily as a mechanism of wealth-based detention, separating defendants based on economic resources rather than risk. Reforms enacted in New Jersey, Illinois, Washington, D.C., and numerous local jurisdictions illustrate that reducing reliance on money bail can improve equity without compromising community safety.

Second, pretrial decision-making should prioritize criminal history over offense severity when assessing risk. Prior convictions emerged as the most powerful and consistent predictor of pretrial rearrest, far outperforming charge severity and bail amount. Continued reliance on offense-based bail schedules is therefore both empirically unjustified and normatively problematic. Shifting the focus toward accumulated criminal history aligns pretrial policy more closely with the actual determinants of risk and with long-standing legal standards emphasizing individualized assessments of danger and flight risk (Stack v. Boyle, 1951).

Third, the use of preventive detention should be narrowly targeted toward defendants with extensive and persistent criminal records. The results indicate that pretrial risk is highly concentrated among repeat offenders with significant prior records. Constraining detention decisions to this narrow group would protect due process, reduce unnecessary incarceration, and allow courts to focus their limited coercive authority on individuals most likely to reoffend.

Fourth, jurisdictions should expand the use of non-monetary conditions of release. Because monetary bail fails to reduce rearrest, courts should rely more heavily on alternatives, including court-date reminders, text-message notifications, transportation assistance, supervised release, and behavioral health interventions. A growing body of research indicates that these measures are more effective than financial conditions at promoting court compliance and public safety (Stevenson, 2018).

Fifth, policymakers should reevaluate the length and scope of pretrial detention. The finding that more extended pretrial detention increases the likelihood of rearrest underscores the criminogenic consequences of incarceration itself. Establishing clearer limits on detention—particularly for low-level and nonviolent defendants—can reduce destabilization, preserve employment and family ties, and ultimately improve both public safety and judicial efficiency.

Finally, the strong association between court-appointed counsel and pretrial rearrest highlights the pervasive role of socioeconomic inequality in pretrial outcomes. Meaningful bail reform, therefore, requires investments beyond the courtroom. Expanding access to housing assistance, employment services, substance-use treatment, and mental health care—particularly through holistic defense models—can mitigate structural disadvantage and improve pretrial performance for economically vulnerable defendants.

Collectively, these reforms would move the pretrial system toward a model grounded in empirical evidence, constitutional values, and fundamental fairness, replacing wealth-based detention with risk-informed, humane, and effective public safety policy.

Study Limitations

While the findings of this study provide important insights into the determinants of pretrial rearrest, several limitations should be acknowledged to contextualize the results and guide their interpretation properly. These limitations do not undermine the central conclusions of the analysis but instead clarify the scope of inference that the data and methods can support.

First, the study relies on administrative data from the State Court Processing Statistics (SCPS) program, restricted to felony defendants from 35 large urban counties that provided complete and comparable data for the variables required in the analysis. Although these counties represent major population centers and account for a substantial share of serious felony case processing in the United States, they do not necessarily reflect court practices, resource environments, or defendant populations in rural or midsize jurisdictions. Consequently, the generalizability of the findings beyond large urban settings should be approached with appropriate caution.

Second, while SCPS provides unusually rich coverage of legal case-processing variables, it lacks direct measures of many individual and contextual factors known to influence pretrial outcomes, including socioeconomic disadvantage, mental health status, substance use, employment stability, social supports, and neighborhood conditions (Lowenkamp et al., 2013). Although the analysis incorporates indirect proxies—such as legal representation type and criminal justice supervision status—these measures cannot fully capture the complexity of defendants' social and economic circumstances.

Third, the primary outcome measure—pretrial rearrest—is itself an imperfect indicator of new criminal activity. Rearrest is shaped not only by offending behavior but also by local policing practices, surveillance intensity, and neighborhood enforcement patterns (Fagan & Davies, 2000). Communities subject to heavier policing—disproportionately communities of color—may therefore exhibit elevated rearrest rates that reflect differential enforcement rather than differential offending. Moreover, the SCPS data do not distinguish between rearrests for new criminal offenses and arrests for technical violations, particularly among individuals under supervision. Because technical violations can substantially inflate rearrest counts without reflecting substantive criminal conduct, this limitation may affect the interpretation of observed pretrial failure rates (Phelps, 2013).

Fourth, the precision of the offense-severity estimates is constrained by the small number of murder cases used as the reference category in the regression models. This choice contributes to larger standard errors for offense comparisons, reducing statistical power to detect differences across offense types even when substantive differences are present. Future research could explore alternative reference categories or employ datasets with more balanced offense distributions.

Fifth, although logistic regression is well suited for modeling dichotomous outcomes, it imposes assumptions regarding the functional form of relationships and the stability of effects across defendants. While extensive diagnostic testing revealed no major violations, the models do not fully account for unobserved heterogeneity at the county or individual level. More flexible approaches—such as hierarchical models or machine learning methods—could better capture jurisdictional variation and nonlinear risk patterns (Hastie et al., 2009).

Finally, the cross-sectional structure of the SCPS data limits causal inference. Although the inclusion of county fixed effects and extensive covariate controls helps mitigate confounding, unobserved policy changes, institutional practices, or shifts in local legal culture may still influence the observed relationships. Longitudinal designs, repeated measures, and natural experiments would strengthen future causal assessments of the effects of pretrial policy.

Despite these limitations, the study provides a robust and internally consistent body of evidence demonstrating that prior criminal convictions remain the most reliable and substantively powerful predictor of pretrial rearrest. Recognizing these boundaries clarifies the contribution of the present analysis while identifying important directions for future research.

Future Research

The limitations identified in this study highlight several important directions for future research on pretrial risk, judicial decision-making, and reform.

First, future analyses should extend beyond large urban jurisdictions to include suburban, rural, and midsized counties. Pretrial practices, resource availability, and case-processing norms vary substantially across geographic contexts, and broader jurisdictional coverage would improve generalizability while revealing how local institutional environments shape pretrial outcomes.

Second, subsequent studies should incorporate richer measures of defendants' social and economic conditions, including mental health status, substance use, employment stability, housing security, and family support. These factors are known to influence both criminal justice involvement and compliance, but are not captured in administrative court datasets such as SCPS. Linking court records with social service, behavioral health, housing, and labor market data would substantially strengthen explanatory and predictive models of pretrial risk.

Third, improving the measurement of pretrial failure represents a critical priority for future work. Distinguishing between new criminal conduct and technical violations would provide a more precise understanding of pretrial misconduct and align empirical research more closely with contemporary policy debates regarding supervision practices and sanctioning. Integrating information on policing intensity, neighborhood conditions, and enforcement strategies would further help disentangle behavioral risk from differential surveillance.

Fourth, future research should continue to advance methodological approaches to studying pretrial outcomes. Multilevel models can account for clustering of defendants within jurisdictions and capture the influence of contextual factors such as judicial culture, local policy regimes, and pretrial services capacity. Time-to-event (survival) analyses can illuminate not only whether but when pretrial failures occur, offering insights into the timing and dynamics of risk. Machine learning techniques may further complement traditional regression by uncovering nonlinear relationships, interaction effects, and complex risk structures that parametric models often overlook.

Fifth, longitudinal research tracking defendants across multiple cases and over extended periods would permit stronger causal inferences regarding the long-term effects of criminal history, supervision status, socioeconomic disadvantage, and pretrial experiences. Natural experiments created by staggered implementation of bail reform policies across jurisdictions provide particularly valuable opportunities for causal evaluation.

Finally, future studies should assess the broader system-level consequences of bail reform, including effects on judicial behavior, jail populations, racial disparities, community stability, and long-term public safety. As jurisdictions continue to restructure their pretrial systems, rigorous empirical evaluation will be essential to ensuring that reforms succeed in reducing unnecessary detention, promoting equity, and protecting public safety.

Together, these research directions offer a roadmap for strengthening the empirical foundation of pretrial policy and extending the contributions of the present study.

Conclusion

This study provides a rigorous, comprehensive assessment of the factors associated with pretrial rearrest among felony defendants in large urban jurisdictions. Across both descriptive and multivariate analyses, prior criminal history consistently emerges as the strongest and most reliable predictor of pretrial failure. These findings directly challenge long-standing assumptions embedded in charge-based bail schedules and monetary bail practices. Once legally relevant and contextual factors are taken into account, neither offense severity nor the financial conditions of release meaningfully predict pretrial misconduct. Instead, accumulated criminal history—particularly prior convictions—dominates the risk landscape.

The results further illuminate the structural forces shaping pretrial outcomes. Socioeconomic disadvantage, supervisory status at arrest, length of pretrial detention, and gender all exert substantial influence on pretrial behavior. Together, these patterns underscore that pretrial failure is not simply a function of the current charge but reflects broader social positioning, system exposure, and institutional practices.

Taken as a whole, the evidence presented in this study supports a fundamental reorientation of pretrial policy. A system grounded in empirical risk indicators rather than monetary thresholds or offense labels offers a more effective, equitable, and constitutionally sound approach to pretrial justice. By reducing reliance on financial conditions, prioritizing validated predictors such as criminal history, and designing policies responsive to the social realities of defendants' lives, jurisdictions can enhance public safety while simultaneously promoting fairness and judicial legitimacy.

As bail reform continues to reshape criminal justice systems across the United States, the findings of this study provide clear, timely, and policy-relevant guidance. Courts, lawmakers, and practitioners seeking to modernize pretrial justice will find in this evidence a strong foundation for building systems that are not only more efficient but also more humane and just.

About the Authors

Enrique Chavez, Ph.D., is a seasoned law enforcement and criminology professional with more than three decades of experience. A retired Police Commander with 32 years of service in a major metropolitan agency, he has held prominent leadership roles in intelligence and terrorism operations and in dignitary protection. He has served as Executive Officer to the Police Chief. His scholarly work has been published in academic journals, and he has held national leadership positions in both Alpha Phi Sigma and the National Latino Peace Officers Association. Dr. Chavez is the CEO of the Chavez Investigative Agency and currently serves as an adjunct professor at South Florida State College.

Stewart J. D'Alessio, Ph.D., is a criminologist and professor at Florida International University (FIU), specializing in criminal justice research. His work focuses on crime trends, sentencing disparities, juvenile delinquency, and the impact of public policies on crime and justice outcomes. Dr. D'Alessio has co-authored numerous studies examining issues such as racial and ethnic disparities in the criminal justice system, gun violence, and the effects of pretrial detention. His research employs quantitative methodologies to analyze crime patterns and inform policy decisions.

Lisa Stolzenberg, Ph.D., is a criminologist and professor known for her research on criminal justice, particularly crime trends, sentencing, and the effects of social policies on crime. She has published extensively on topics such as gun control, juvenile delinquency, and racial disparities in the criminal justice system. Dr. Stolzenberg is a faculty member at Florida International University

(FIU) and has contributed significantly to the field through empirical studies that analyze crime patterns and the effectiveness of policies.

References

Agan, A., & Starr, S. (2018). Ban the box, criminal records, and racial discrimination: A field experiment. *The Quarterly Journal of Economics, 133*(1), 191–235.

Agnew, R. (2017). Building on the foundation of general strain theory: Specifying the types of strain most likely to lead to crime and delinquency. In *Recent developments in criminological theory* (pp. 311–354). Routledge.

Agresti, A. (2018). *An introduction to categorical data analysis* (3rd ed.). Wiley.

Albonetti, C. A. (1989). Bail and judicial discretion in the District of Columbia. *Sociology and Social Research, 74*(1), 40–47.

Allen, J. A. (2016). Making bail: Limiting the use of bail schedules and defining the elusive meaning of excessive bail. *Journal of Law and Policy, 25*, 637–669.

Allison, P. D. (2001). *Missing data*. Sage Publications.

Ansel, N. (2021). Advancing criminal reform through ballot initiatives. *Arizona State Law Journal, 53*(1), 273–331.

Anwar, S., Bushway, S., & Engberg, J. (2023). The impact of defense counsel at bail hearings. *Science Advances, 9*(18), eade3909. https://doi.org/10.1126/sciadv.ade3909

Bachman, R., & Schutt, R. K. (2020). *The practice of research in criminology and criminal justice* (7th ed.). Sage.

Barmaki, R. (2019). On the origin of "labeling" theory in criminology: Frank Tannenbaum and the Chicago School of Sociology. *Deviant Behavior, 40*(2), 256–271.

Barno, M., Martínez, D. N., & Williams, K. R. (2020). Exploring alternatives to cash bail: An evaluation of Orange County's pretrial assessment and release supervision (PARS) program. *American Journal of Criminal Justice, 45*, 363–378.

Bearfield, D., Humphrey, N., Portillo, S., & Riccucci, N. (2023). Dismantling institutional and structural racism:

Implementation strategies across the United States. *Journal of Social Equity and Public Administration, 1*(1), 75-92.

Bechtel, K., Clark, J., Jones, M. R., & Levin, D. J. (2012). *Dispelling the myths: What policymakers need to know about pretrial research*. Pretrial Justice Institute.

Bechtel, K., Lowenkamp, C. T., & Holsinger, A. (2011). Identifying the predictors of pretrial failure: A meta-analysis. *Federal Probation, 75*, 78–87.

Beck, A. J., Berzofsky, M., Caspar, R., & Krebs, C. (2013). *Sexual victimization in prisons and jails reported by inmates, 2011– 12* (NCJ 241399). Bureau of Justice Statistics, U.S. Department of Justice.

Becker, H. S. (1963). *Outsiders: Studies in the sociology of deviance*. Free Press Glencoe.

Belsley, D. A., Kuh, E., & Welsch, R. E. (1980). *Regression diagnostics: Identifying influential data and sources of collinearity*. Wiley.

Bernburg, J. G., Krohn, M. D., & Rivera, C. J. (2006). Official labeling, criminal embeddedness, and subsequent delinquency: A longitudinal test of labeling theory. *Journal of Research in Crime and Delinquency, 43*(1), 67–88.

Boutwell, A. E., Allen, S. A., & Rich, J. D. (2005). Opportunities to address the hepatitis C epidemic in the correctional setting. *Clinical Infectious Diseases, 40*(Suppl. 5), S367–S372.

Box, G. E. P., & Tidwell, P. W. (1962). Transformation of the independent variables. *Technometrics, 4*(4), 531–550. https://doi.org/10.1080/00401706.1962.10490038

Boyd, C. L. (2016). Representation on the courts? The effects of trial judges' sex and race. *Political Research Quarterly, 69*(4), 788–799.

Brooker, C. M. (2017). *Yakima County, Washington pretrial justice system improvements: Pre- and post-implementation analysis*.

Buehler, E. D. (2021). *Sexual victimization reported by adult correctional authorities, 2016–2018*. U.S. Department of Justice, Bureau of Justice Statistics.

https://bjs.ojp.gov/sites/g/files/xyckuh236/files/media/document/svraca1618.pdf

Bureau of Justice Statistics. (2014). *State Court Processing Statistics, 1990–2009: Felony defendants in large urban counties*. Inter-university Consortium for Political and Social Research [distributor], 2014-06-24. https://doi.org/10.3886/ICPSR02038.v5

Cahalan, M. W. (1986). *Historical corrections statistics in the United States*. U.S. Department of Justice, Bureau of Justice Statistics.

Calaway, W. R., & Kinsley, J. M. (2018). Rethinking bail reform. *University of Richmond Law Review, 52*, 795–828.

Campbell, M. C., & Vogel, M. (2019). The demographic divide: Population dynamics, race, and the rise of mass incarceration in the United States. *Punishment & Society, 21*(1), 47–69.

Caravaca-Sánchez, F., & Wolff, N. (2016). Prevalence and predictors of sexual victimization among incarcerated men and women in Spanish prisons. *Criminal Justice and Behavior, 43*(8), 977–991.

Carlucci, W. M. (2019). Death of a bail bondsman: The implementation and successes of nonmonetary, risk-based bail systems. *Emory Law Journal, 69*(6), 1205–1253.

Carroll, J. E. (2020). The due process of bail. *Wake Forest Law Review, 55*, 757–792.

Carroll, M. (2021). *Pretrial release and supervision*. National Conference of State Legislatures. https://www.ncsl.org/civil-and-criminal-justice/pretrial-release-and-supervision

Charles, P., Muentner, L., Jensen, S., Packard, C., Haimson, C., Eason, J., & Poehlmann-Tynan, J. (2022). Incarcerated during a pandemic: Implications of COVID-19 for jailed individuals and their families. *Corrections, 7*(5), 357–368.

Cherson, J. (2022a). *Policy position brief: On electronic monitoring*. The Bail Project. https://bailproject.org/policy/electronic-monitoring/#:~:text=Given%20the%20lack%20of%20data,condition%2C%20or%20combination%20of%20conditions%2C

Cherson, J. (2022b). *Policy position brief: On pretrial algorithms*. The Bail Project. https://bailproject.org/policy/pretrial-algorithms/#:~:text=Pretrial%20algorithms%20are%20problematic%20because,legal%20system%20is%20predicated%20upon

Chiricos, T., Barrick, K., Bales, W., & Bontrager, S. (2007). The labeling of convicted felons and its consequences for recidivism. *Criminology, 45*(3), 547–581.

Clear, T. R. (2007). The impacts of incarceration on public safety. *Social Research: An International Quarterly, 74*(2), 613–630.

Coggins, E. A. (2020). An overview of the bail system in the United States and its discriminatory components. *The Mid-Southern Journal of Criminal Justice, 1*(1), 3.

Cohen, J., Cohen, P., West, S. G., & Aiken, L. S. (2003). *Applied multiple regression/correlation analysis for the behavioral sciences* (3rd ed.). Lawrence Erlbaum Associates.

Cohen, T. H., & Reaves, B. A. (2007). *State court processing statistics, 1990–2004: Pretrial release of felony defendants in state courts*. U.S. Department of Justice.

Colbert, D. L., Paternoster, R., & Bushway, S. (2002). Do attorneys really matter? The empirical and legal case for the right to counsel at bail. *Cardozo Law Review, 23*, 1719–1793.

Conklin, S. (2011). Juveniles locked in limbo: Why pretrial detention implicates a fundamental right. *Minnesota Law Review, 96*, 2150 2181.

Cooley, C. H. (1902). *Human nature and social order*. Scribners.

Copp, J. E., Casey, W., Blomberg, T. G., & Pesta, G. (2022). Pretrial risk assessment instruments in practice: The role of judicial discretion in pretrial reform. *Criminology & Public Policy, 21*(2), 329–358.

Cornelius, G. F. (2012). Jails: Pretrial detention and short-term confinement. In *The Oxford handbook of sentencing and corrections* (pp. 389–415). Oxford University Press.

Dabney, D. A., Page, J., & Topalli, V. (2017). American bail and the tinting of criminal justice. *The Howard Journal of Crime and Justice, 56*(4), 397–418.

D'Alessio, S. J., Stolzenberg, L., & Flexon, J. L. (2014). The effect of Hawaii's ban-the-box law on repeat offending. *American Journal of Criminal Justice, 40*, 336–352.

D'Alessio, S. J., & Stolzenberg, L. (2021). Higher money bail doesn't lead to greater public safety. *The Crime Report.* The Center on Media, Crime, and Justice at John Jay College.

Davis, D. (2022). Care of justice-involved populations. *Missouri Medicine, 119*(3), 208–212.

Demuth, S. (2003). Racial and ethnic differences in pretrial release decisions and outcomes: A comparison of Hispanic, Black, and White felony arrestees. *Criminology, 41*(3), 873–908.

Demuth, S., & Steffensmeier, D. (2004). The impact of gender and race-ethnicity in the pretrial release process. *Social Problems, 51*(2), 222–242.

Denver, M., Pickett, J. T., & Bushway, S. D. (2018). Criminal records and employment: A survey of experiences and attitudes in the United States. *Justice Quarterly, 35*(4), 584–613.

Desmarais, S. L., & Lowder, E. M. (2019). *Pretrial risk assessment tools: A primer for judges, prosecutors, and defense attorneys.* Safety and Justice Challenge.

Digard, L., & Swavola, E. (2019). *Justice denied: The harmful and lasting effects of pretrial detention.* Vera Institute of Justice.

Dobbie, W., Goldin, J., & Yang, C. S. (2018). The effects of pretrial detention on conviction, future crime, and employment: Evidence from randomly assigned judges. *American Economic Review, 108*(2), 201–240.

Dobbie, W., & Yang, C. S. (2021). The U.S. pretrial system: Balancing individual rights and public interests. *Journal of Economic Perspectives, 35*(4), 49–70.

Donnelly, E. A., & MacDonald, J. M. (2018). The downstream effects of bail and pretrial detention on racial disparities in incarceration. *Journal of Criminal Law & Criminology, 108*(4), 775–814.

Fagan, J., & Davies, G. (2000). Street stops and broken windows: Terry, race, and disorder in New York City. *Fordham Urban Law Journal, 28*(2), 457–504.

Fair, H., & Walmsley, R. (2016). *World prison population list* (13th ed.). Institute for Criminal Policy Research. https://www.prisonstudies.org/sites/default/files/resources /downloads/world_prison_population_list_13th_edition.pdf

Favril, L., Yu, R., Hawton, K., & Fazel, S. (2020). Risk factors for self-harm in prison: A systematic review and meta-analysis. *The Lancet Psychiatry, 7*(8), 682–691.

Fazel, S., & Baillargeon, J. (2011). The health of prisoners. *The Lancet, 377*(9769), 956–965.

Feeley, M. M. (1983). *Court reform on trial: Why simple solutions fail.* Basic Books.

Fishbane, A., Ouss, A., & Shah, A. K. (2020). Behavioral nudges reduce failure to appear for court. *Science, 370*(6517), eabb6591.

Futrell, N. S. (2020). Decarcerating New York City: Lessons from a pandemic. *Fordham Urban Law Journal, 48*(1), 57–94.

Garrett, B. L. (2022). Models of bail reform. *Florida Law Review.* http://www.floridalawreview.com/wp-content/uploads/1_Garrett.pdf

Gase, L. N., Glenn, B. A., Gomez, L. M., Kuo, T., Inkelas, M., & Ponce, N. A. (2016). Understanding racial and ethnic disparities in arrest: The role of individual, family, and neighborhood factors. *Crime & Delinquency, 62*(4), 446–473. https://doi.org/10.1177/0011128713492495

Gideon v. Wainwright, 372 U.S. 335 (1963).

Goldkamp, J. S. (1980). The effects of detention on judicial decisions: A closer look. *The Justice System Journal, 5*(3), 234–257.

Gottfredson, D. M., & Gottfredson, S. D. (1988). Stakes and risks in the prediction of violent criminal behavior. *Violence and Victims, 3*(4), 247–263.

Gottfredson, M. R., & Hirschi, T. (1990). *A general theory of crime.* Stanford University Press.

Gross, J. (2018). Devil take the hindmost: Reform considerations for states with a constitutional right to bail. *Akron Law Review, 52*, 1043–1080.

Gustafson, K. S. (2011). *Cheating welfare: Public assistance and the criminalization of poverty*. New York University Press.

Hagan, J. (1993). The social embeddedness of crime and unemployment. *Criminology, 31*(4), 465–491.

Hammett, T. M. (2009). Sexually transmitted diseases and incarceration. *Current Opinion in Infectious Diseases, 22*(1), 77–81.

Hansen, M. H. (2010). Democratic freedom and the concept of freedom in Plato and Aristotle. *Greek, Roman, and Byzantine Studies, 50*(1), 1–27.

Hanson, R. A. (2003). *Indigent defense services in the United States, 1999*. Bureau of Justice Statistics. https://bjs.ojp.gov/content/pub/pdf/idsu99.pdf

Harlow, C. W. (2000). *Defense counsel in criminal cases* (NCJ 179023). Bureau of Justice Statistics, U.S. Department of Justice. https://bjs.ojp.gov/content/pub/pdf/dccc.pdf

Harris, A., Evans, H., & Beckett, K. (2010). Drawing blood from stones: Legal debt and social inequality in the contemporary United States. *American Journal of Sociology, 115*(6), 1753–1799.

Hastie, T., Tibshirani, R., & Friedman, J. (2009). *The elements of statistical learning: Data mining, inference, and prediction* (2nd ed.). Springer.

Hatton, R., & Smith, J. (2020). Research on the effectiveness of pretrial support and supervision services: A guide for pretrial services programs. *UNC School of Government Criminal Justice Innovation Lab*.

Heaton, P., Mayson, S., & Stevenson, M. (2017). The downstream consequences of misdemeanor pretrial detention. *Stanford Law Review, 69*, 711–794.

Hegreness, M. J. (2013). America's fundamental and vanishing right to bail. *Arizona Law Review, 55*, 909–996.

Henning, K. (2022). Inconsistencies in Bail Determinations: An Analysis of Judicial Decision-Making. *Ind. JL & Soc. Equal., 10*, 437.

Hirschi, T. (1969). *Causes of delinquency*. University of California Press.

Hochstetler, A., Copes, H., & DeLisi, M. (2002). Differential association in group and solo offending. *Journal of Criminal Justice, 30*(6), 559–566.

Holsinger, A. M., & Holsinger, K. (2018). Analyzing bond supervision survey data: The effects of pretrial detention on self-reported outcomes. *Federal Probation, 82*, 39–44.

Hosmer, D. W., Lemeshow, S., & Sturdivant, R. X. (2013). *Applied logistic regression* (3rd ed.). Wiley.

Howat, H., Forsyth, C. J., Biggar, R., & Howat, S. (2016). Improving court-appearance rates through court-date reminder phone calls. *Criminal Justice Studies, 29*(1), 77–87. https://doi.org/10.1080/1478601X.2015.1121875

Hurley, G. (2016). *The constitutionality of bond schedules*. National Center for State Courts.

IBM Corp. (2017). *IBM SPSS Statistics for Windows* (Version 25) [Computer software]. IBM Corp.

Jannetta, J., & Duane, M. (2022). *Risk assessment and structured decision-making for pretrial release*. Urban Institute.

Johnson, L. M., Simons, R. L., & Conger, R. D. (2004). Criminal justice system involvement and continuity of youth crime: A longitudinal analysis. *Youth & Society, 36*(1), 3–29.

Jones, M. R. (2013). *Unsecured bonds: The as effective and most efficient pretrial release option*. Pretrial Justice Institute.

Kaeble, D., & Cowhig, M. (2018). *Correctional populations in the United States, 2016*. U.S. Department of Justice, Bureau of Justice Statistics.

Katz, C. M., & Spohn, C. C. (1995). The effect of race and gender on bail outcomes: A test of an interactive model. *American Journal of Criminal Justice, 19*, 161–184.

Kennedy, S., House, L., & Williams, M. (2013). Using research to improve pretrial justice and public safety: Results from PSA's risk assessment validation project. *Federal Probation, 77*(2), 28–34.

Kincaid, R. (2023). Mass incarceration and misinformation: The COVID-19 infodemic behind bars. *University of St. Thomas Law Journal, 19*(2), 323–352.

Kleck, G., & Barnes, J. C. (2010). Do more police lead to more crime deterrence? The evidence from U.S. cities. *International Journal of Police Science & Management, 12*(3), 287–297. https://doi.org/10.1350/ijps.2010.12.3.189

Klein, D. J. (1997). The pretrial detention crisis: The causes and the cure. *Urban Law Annual/Journal of Urban and Contemporary Law, 52*, 281–306.

Koepke, J. L., & Robinson, D. G. (2018). Danger ahead: Risk assessment and the future of bail reform. *Washington Law Review, 93*, 1725–1807.

Kolbeck, S. G., Bellair, P. E., & Lopez, S. (2022). Race, work history, and the employment–recidivism relationship. *Criminology, 60*(4), 637–666.

Kopak, A. M., & Singer, A. J. (2023). Substance use disorder, bail reform, and failure to appear in court: Results from a naturalistic study. *Journal of Drug Issues, 53*(2), 183–195. https://doi.org/10.1177/00220426221150094

Koppel, S., Bergin, T., Ropac, R., Randolph, I., & Joseph, H. (2022). Examining the causal effect of pretrial detention on case outcomes: A judge fixed effect instrumental variable approach. *Journal of Experimental Criminology*, 1–18.

Lageson, S., Vuolo, M., & Uggen, C. (2015). Legal ambiguity in managerial assessments of criminal records. *Law & Social Inquiry, 40*, 175–204.

LaLonde, R., & Cho, R. (2008). The impact of incarceration in state prison on the employment prospects of women. *Journal of Quantitative Criminology, 24*, 243–265.

Lemert, E. M. (1951). *Social pathology: A systematic approach to the theory of sociopathic behavior*.

Lerman, A. E., Green, A. L., & Dominguez, P. (2022). Pleading for justice: Bullpen therapy, pretrial detention, and plea bargains in American courts. *Crime & Delinquency, 68*(2), 159–182.

Leslie, E., & Pope, N. G. (2017). The unintended impact of pretrial detention on case outcomes: Evidence from New York City arraignments. *The Journal of Law and Economics, 60*(3), 529–557.

Lessnick, J. M. (2022). Pretrial detention by a preponderance: The constitutional and interpretive shortcomings of the flight-risk standard. *University of Chicago Law Review, 89*(5), 1245–1288.

Liu, P., Nunn, R., & Shambaugh, J. (2018). *The economics of bail and pretrial detention*. Economic Analysis. https://nyapsa.org/assets/files/BailFineReform_EA_121818_6PM.pdf

Long, J. S., & Freese, J. (2014). *Regression models for categorical dependent variables using Stata* (3rd ed.). Stata Press.

Louis, S. S. (2022). Bail denied or bail too high? Disentangling cumulative disadvantage by pretrial detention type. *Journal of Criminal Justice, 82*, 101971.

Lowder, E. M., Diaz, C. L., Grommon, E., & Ray, B. R. (2021). Effects of pretrial risk assessments on release decisions and misconduct outcomes relative to practice as usual. *Journal of Criminal Justice, 73*, 101754.

Lowenkamp, C. T., & Bechtel, K. (2009). *Meeting pretrial objectives: A validation of the Summit County pretrial risk assessment instrument (SCPRAI)*. Unpublished manuscript.

Lowenkamp, C. T., VanNostrand, M., & Holsinger, A. M. (2013). *The hidden costs of pretrial detention*. Laura & John Arnold Foundation.

Lynch, M. J., & Patterson, E. B. (1991). *Race and criminal justice*. Harrow and Heston.

Maruna, S. (2001). *Making good*. American Psychological Association.

Massoglia, M., & Pridemore, W. A. (2015). Incarceration and health. *Annual Review of Sociology, 41*, 291–310.

McEachin, A., Lauen, D. L., Fuller, S. C., & Perera, R. M. (2020). Social returns to private choice? Effects of charter schools on behavioral outcomes, arrests, and civic participation. *Economics of Education Review, 76*, 101–122.

McGovern, V., Demuth, S., & Jacoby, J. E. (2009). Racial and ethnic recidivism risks: A comparison of postincarceration rearrest, reconviction, and reincarceration among White, Black, and Hispanic releasees. *The Prison Journal, 89*(3), 309–327.

Menard, S. (2010). *Logistic regression: From introductory to advanced concepts and applications*. Sage Publications.

Metzner, J. L., & Hayes, L. M. (2020). Jails and prisons. In L. H. Gold & R. L. Fierson (Eds.), *The American Psychiatric Association publishing textbook of suicide risk assessment and management* (3rd ed., pp. 265–281). American Psychiatric Association Publishing.

Minton, T. D., & Zeng, Z. (2016). *Jail inmates in 2015*. U.S. Department of Justice, Bureau of Justice Statistics.

Minton, T. D., & Zeng, Z. (2021). *Jail inmates in 20—Statistical tables*. U.S. Department of Justice, Bureau of Justice Statistics.

Mitchell, O., Mora, D. O., Sticco, T. L., & Boggess, L. N. (2022). Are progressive chief prosecutors effective in reducing prison use and cumulative racial/ethnic disadvantage? Evidence from Florida. *Criminology & Public Policy, 21*(3), 535–565.

Monaghan, J., van Holm, E. J., & Surprenant, C. W. (2022). Get jailed, jump bail? The impacts of cash bail on failure to appear and rearrest in Orleans Parish. *American Journal of Criminal Justice, 47*(1), 56–74.

Moody-Ramirez, M., Tait, G., & Bland, D. (2021). An analysis of George Floyd-themed memes: A Critical Race Theory approach to analyzing memes surrounding the 2020 George Floyd protests. *The Journal of Social Media in Society, 10*(2), 373–401.

Moore, K. (2022). *Pretrial justice without money bail or risk assessments*. Thurgood Marshall Institute.

https://tminstituteldf.org/wp-content/uploads/2022/01/TMI_PretrialJusticeWithoutCBorRA2.pdf

Motz, R. T., Barnes, J. C., Caspi, A., Arseneault, L., Cullen, F. T., Houts, R., Wertz, J., & Moffitt, T. E. (2020). Does contact with the justice system deter or promote future delinquency? Results from a longitudinal study of British adolescent twins. *Criminology, 58*(2), 307–335. https://doi.org/10.1111/1745-9125.12236

Murtha, M. (2024). Warning: Civil rights in California may vary by county due to unconstitutional bail schedules. *University of the Pacific Law Review, 55*(2), 313–340.

Nagel, I. H. (1982). The legal/extra-legal controversy: Judicial decisions in pretrial release. *Law & Society Review, 17*, 481–515.

Nagin, D. S., & Pogarsky, G. (2001). Integrating celerity, impulsivity, and extralegal sanction threats into a model of general deterrence: Theory and evidence. *Criminology, 39*(4), 865–892. https://doi.org/10.1111/j.1745-9125.2001.tb00943.x

O'Brien, R. M. (2007). A caution regarding rules of thumb for variance inflation factors. *Quality & Quantity, 41*(5), 673–690. https://doi.org/10.1007/s11135-006-9018-6

O'Donnell v. Harris County, Texas, 882 F.3d 528 (5th Cir. 2018).

Ottone, S., & Scott-Hayward, C. S. (2018). Pretrial detention and the decision to impose bail in Southern California. *Criminology, Criminal Justice, Law & Society, 19*, 24–45.

Ouss, A., & Stevenson, M. (2023). Does cash bail deter misconduct? *American Economic Journal: Applied Economics, 15*(3), 150–182.

Pager, D. (2003). The mark of a criminal record. *American Journal of Sociology, 108*(5), 937–975.

Pager, D. (2008). *Marked: Race, crime, and finding work in an era of mass incarceration*. University of Chicago Press.

Petersen, N. (2020). Do detainees plead guilty faster? A survival analysis of pretrial detention and the timing of guilty pleas. *Criminal Justice Policy Review, 31*(7), 1015–1035.

Pettit, B., & Lyons, C. J. (2007). Status and the stigma of incarceration: The labor market effects of incarceration by race, class, and criminal involvement. In S. Bushway, M. A. Stoll, & D. F. Weiman (Eds.), *The labor market for released prisoners in post-industrial America* (pp. 203–226). Russell Sage Foundation.

Phelps, M. S. (2013). The paradox of probation: Community supervision in the age of mass incarceration. *Law & Policy, 35*(1–2), 51–80. https://doi.org/10.1111/lapo.12002

Piquero, A. R., Farrington, D. P., & Blumstein, A. (2015). Key issues in criminal careers research—2014 revision. In A. R. Piquero (Ed.), *The handbook of criminological theory* (2nd ed., pp. 96–114). Wiley.

Pryce, D. K., & Gainey, R. (2022). Race differences in public satisfaction with and trust in the local police in the context of George Floyd protests: An analysis of residents' experiences and attitudes. *Criminal Justice Studies, 35*(1), 74–92.

Puglisi, L. B., Brinkley-Rubinstein, L., & Wang, E. A. (2023). COVID-19 in carceral systems: A review. *Annual Review of Criminology, 6*(1), 399–422.

Reaves, B. A. (2013). *Felony defendants in large urban counties, 2009.* U.S. Department of Justice, Bureau of Justice Statistics.

Redcross, C., Henderson, B., Miratrix, L., & Valentine, E. (2019). *Evaluation of pretrial justice system reforms that use the public safety assessment: Effects in Mecklenburg County, North Carolina.* MDRC Center for Criminal Justice Research. https://www.mdrc.org/sites/default/files/PSA_Mecklenburg _Brief2.pdf

Rice, M. E., & Harris, G. T. (2005). Comparing effect sizes in follow-up studies: ROC area, Cohen's d, and r. *Law and Human Behavior, 29*(5), 615–620. https://doi.org/10.1007/s10979-005-6832-7

Rose, E. K., & Shem-Tov, Y. (2021). How does incarceration affect reoffending? Estimating the dose-response function. *Journal of Political Economy, 129*(12), 3302–3356.

Rowan, Z. R., Fine, A., Steinberg, L., Frick, P. J., & Cauffman, E. (2023). Labeling effects of initial juvenile justice system processing decision on youth interpersonal ties. *Criminology, 61*(4), 731–757.

Rowell-Cunsolo, T. L., Szeto, B., Sampong, S. A., & Larson, E. L. (2016). Predictors of sexual behaviour among men and women in New York City area prisons. *Culture, Health & Sexuality, 18*(12), 1393–1406.

Sampson, R. J., & Laub, J. H. (1993). *Crime in the making: Pathways and turning points through life*. Harvard University Press.

Sandberg, M. (2023). The presumption of wealthiness: How the current bail system in Minnesota is problematically classist. *Mitchell Hamline Law Review, 49*(1), 58–91.

Sawyer, W. (2019). How race impacts who is detained pretrial. *Prison Policy Initiative.* https://www.prisonpolicy.org/blog/2019/10/09/pretrial_rac e/#:~:text=Nearly%207%20in%2010%20(69,of%20the%20to tal%20U.S.%20population

Sawyer, W., & Wagner, P. (2023). *Mass incarceration: The whole pie 2023*. Prison Policy Initiative. https://www.prisonpolicy.org/reports/pie2023.html

Schlesinger, T. (2005). Racial and ethnic disparity in pretrial criminal processing. *Justice Quarterly, 22*(2), 170–192.

Schnacke, T. R. (2014). *Fundamentals of bail: A resource guide for pretrial practitioners and a framework for American pretrial reform*. National Institute of Corrections.

Schnacke, T. R., Jones, M. R., & Brooker, C. M. (2010). *The history of bail and pretrial release*. Pretrial Justice Institute.

Schnacke, T. R., Jones, M. R., & Wilderman, D. M. (2012). Increasing court-appearance rates and other benefits of live-caller telephone court-date reminders: The Jefferson County, Colorado, FTA pilot project and resulting court date notification program. *Connecticut Review, 48*, 86–110.

Schnittker, J., Massoglia, M., & Uggen, C. (2011). Incarceration and the health of the African American community. *Du Bois Review, 8*(1), 1–9.

Schwartzapfel, B., Park, K., & Demillo, A. (2020). 1 in 5 prisoners in the U.S. has had COVID-19. *The Marshall Project.* https://www.themarshallproject.org/2020/12/18/1-in-5-prisoners-in-the-u-s-has-had-covid-19

Scott-Hayward, C. S., & Fradella, H. F. (2019). The origins and history of bail in the common law tradition. In *Punishing poverty* (pp. 1–31). University of California Press.

Seibler, J. M., & Snead, J. (2017). *The history of cash bail*. Heritage Foundation.

Sherman, L. W. (1993). Defiance, deterrence, and irrelevance: A theory of the criminal sanction. *Journal of Research in Crime and Delinquency, 30*(4), 445–473.

Smith, S. S., & Robson, C. (2022). *Between a rock and a hard place: The social costs of pretrial electronic monitoring in San Francisco.*

Stack v. Boyle, 342 U.S. 1 (1951).

Steadman, H. J., Osher, F. C., Robbins, P. C., Case, B., & Samuels, S. (2009). Prevalence of serious mental illness among jail inmates. *Psychiatric Services, 60*(6), 761–765.

Stephan, J. J. (1984). *The 1983 jail census*. U.S. Department of Justice, Bureau of Justice Statistics.

Stemen, D., & Olson, D. (2023, January). *Is bail reform causing an increase in crime?* Harry Frank Guggenheim Foundation.

Steffensmeier, D., Schwartz, J., Zhong, H., & Ackerman, J. (2005). An assessment of recent trends in girls' violence using diverse longitudinal sources: Is the gender gap closing? *Criminology, 43*(2), 355–406. https://doi.org/10.1111/j.0011-1348.2005.00013.x

Stevenson, M. T. (2018). Distortion of justice: How the inability to pay bail affects case outcomes. *The Journal of Law, Economics, and Organization, 34*(4), 511–542.

Stevenson, M. T., & Mayson, S. G. (2017). Pretrial detention and bail. In E. Luna (Ed.), *Academy for Justice: A report on scholarship and criminal justice reform* (University of Pennsylvania Law School, Public Law Research Paper No. 17-18).

Stolzenberg, L., D'Alessio, S. J., & Flexon, J. L. (2021). The usual suspects: Prior criminal record and the probability of arrest. *Police Quarterly, 24*(1), 31–54.

Struckman-Johnson, C., & Struckman-Johnson, D. (2002). Sexual coercion reported by women in three Midwestern prisons. *Journal of Sex Research, 39*(3), 217–227.

Struckman-Johnson, C., Struckman-Johnson, D., Rucker, L., Bumby, K., & Donaldson, S. (1996). Sexual coercion reported by men and women in prison. *Journal of Sex Research, 33*(1), 67–76.

Subramanian, R., Delaney, R, Roberts, S., Fishman, N., & McGarry, P. (2015). *Incarceration's front door: The misuse of jails in America*. Vera Institute of Justice. https://www.vera.org/publications/incarcerations-front-door-the-misuse-of-jails-in-america

Sutherland, E. H. (1947). *Principles of criminology* (4th ed.). J. B. Lippincott.

Sweeten, G., Piquero, A. R., & Steinberg, L. (2013). Age and the explanation of crime, revisited. *Journal of Youth and Adolescence, 42*(6), 921–938.

Tannenbaum, F. (1938). *Crime and the community*. Columbia University Press.

Tartaro, C., & Sedelmaier, C. M. (2009). A tale of two counties: The impact of pretrial release, race, and ethnicity upon sentencing decisions. *Criminal Justice Studies, 22*(2), 203–221.

Tonry, M. (1994). Racial politics, racial disparities, and the war on crime. *Crime & Delinquency, 40*(4), 475–494.

Travis, J., Western, B., & Redburn, F. S. (2014). *The growth of incarceration in the United States: Exploring causes and consequences*. https://academicworks.cuny.edu/cgi/viewcontent.cgi?article=1026&context=jj_pubs

Turney, K. (2021). Inequalities in jail incarceration across the life course. *Proceedings of the National Academy of Sciences, 118*(19), e2104744118.

Tyler, T. R. (2003). Procedural justice, legitimacy, and the effective rule of law. *Crime and Justice, 30*, 283–357.

Uggen, C., Schnittker, J., Shannon, S., & Massoglia, M. (2023). The contingent effect of incarceration on state health outcomes. *SSM – Population Health, 21*, 101322.

United States v. Salerno, 481 U.S. 739 (1987).

Wang, E. A., Western, B., Backes, E. P., & Schuck, J. (2021). *Decarcerating correctional facilities during COVID-19.*

Warren, C. (2023). *The negative effect of criminal labeling on community reentry in the Harrisonburg area.*

Washington, M. (2021). *Beyond jails: Community-based strategies for public safety.* Vera Institute of Justice.

Western, B. (2006). *Punishment and inequality in America.* Russell Sage Foundation.

Western, B., & Pettit, B. (2010). Incarceration and social inequality. *Daedalus, 139*(3), 8–19.

Wildeman, C., Fitzpatrick, M. D., & Goldman, A. W. (2018). Conditions of confinement in American prisons and jails. *Annual Review of Law and Social Science, 14*, 29–47.

Wilson, A. (2022). Just a misdemeanor: Seeking justice in all cases. *Criminal Justice, 37*(1), 30–33.

Wilson, J. R. (1925, March 12). Education of the public: Necessity for carrying the gospel of corporate suretyship to the financial and business public in every village, town, and city. *The Spectator*, 29.

Wilson, V., & Darity, W., Jr. (2022). *Understanding Black–White disparities in labor market outcomes requires models that account for persistent discrimination and unequal bargaining power.* Economic Policy Institute.

Winicov, N. (2019). A systematic review of behavioral health interventions for suicidal and self-harming individuals in prisons and jails. *Heliyon, 5*(9), e02379.

Wooldredge, J., Frank, J., Goulette, N., & Travis, L., III. (2015). Is the impact of cumulative disadvantage on sentencing greater for Black defendants? *Criminology & Public Policy, 14*(2), 187–223.

World Health Organization. (2021). *Coronavirus disease (COVID-19): How is it transmitted?* https://www.who.int/news-room/questions-and-answers/item/coronavirus-disease-covid-19-how-is-it-transmitted

Yang, C. S. (2017). Toward an optimal bail system. *New York University Law Review, 92*, 1399–1492.

Young, A. (2003). *The minds of marginalized Black men: Making sense of mobility, opportunity, and future life chances.* Princeton University Press.

Zeng, Z. (2022). *Jail inmates in 2021 – Statistical tables.* U.S. Department of Justice, Bureau of Justice Statistics.

Zottola, S. A., Duhart-Clarke, S. E., & Desmarais, S. L. (2021). Bail reform in the United States: The what, why, and how of third wave efforts. In E. Jeglic & C. Calkins (Eds.), *Handbook of issues in criminal justice reform in the United States.* Springer.

Zottola, S. A., Crozier, W. E., Ariturk, D., & Desmarais, S. L. (2023a). Court date reminders reduce court nonappearance: A meta-analysis. *Criminology & Public Policy, 22*(1), 97–123.

Zottola, S. A., Desmarais, S. L., Stewart, D. K., Duhart Clarke, S. E., & Monahan, J. (2023b). Pretrial risk assessment, release recommendations, and racial bias. *Criminal Justice and Behavior, 50*(9), 1255–1278. https://doi.org/10.1177/00938548231174908

www.ingramcontent.com/pod-product-compliance
Lightning Source LLC
Chambersburg PA
CBHW040125270326
41926CB00001B/20